Words of Wisdom

By

Wyllene B. Wall

Small Fish Big Sea Publications
September 2009

Wyllene B. Wall

Small Fish Big Sea Publications
Paperback Book

Publisher's Notes

All rights reserved. No part of this book may be reproduced or transmitted in any form or by any means, electronic or mechanical, including photocopying, recording, or by any information storage and retrieval system, without permission in writing from the publisher.

First Printing

Copyright © 2009 by Wyllene B. Wall

Printed in the United States of America

ISBN: 978-0-9801470-2-5

Cover Design by N'DigoDesign

ACKNOWLEDGMENTS

THANK YOU!

- Soror Belva Denmark Tibbs, for suggesting "Words of Wisdom" as a title.

- Soror Kimberly McKenzie for book formatting and arrangement of the material.

- Soror Barbara Williamson for a final reading and suggestions.

- My beloved husband John and my one and only capable and loving son.

- Steven L. Wall for inspiration and help.

- My best friend Yvonne Gooch for her optimism.

- Soror Mildred Gardner for her encouragement and advice.

- Mary L. Jackson my cousin/sister who never lets me forget.

- All my precious grandchildren, Steve Jr. Freddie, Ebone'. Tyler and Taylor.

- Members of St. Paul UMC and Aldersgate UMC.

- Bishop Julius C. Trimble and family.

TABLE OF CONTENTS

- Biographical Data Wyllene B. Wall
  Pages 7 - 8

- Special Tributes to Wyllene B. Wall
  Pages 9 - 18

- The Wonderful Sorority of Alpha Kappa Alpha (AKA)
  Pages 19 - 86

- A Few Short Stories
  Pages 87 – 102

- Church
  Pages 103 - 151

- Tributes
  Pages 152 - 187

- My Special Poems, Philosophy & Words
  Pages 188 - 258

(Note: Works are categorized by subject, not by date)

WORDS OF WISDOM

'Words of Wisdom' is a personal collection of my writings throughout the years. My life experiences have been plentiful and I leave my 'words of wisdom' for my family, friends and for those who I have had the pleasure of knowing. In this book, you will find poetry, short stories and tributes for what I cherish most: church, family, friends and my sorority, Alpha Kappa Alpha Sorority, Incorporated.

BIOGRAPHICAL DATA WYLLENE BROWNE WALL

Wyllene Browne Wall is the only child of Bessie Sharpe Browne and William Browne. She always wished for brothers and sisters and she found them when she married John L. Wall who has two brothers and two sisters. John and Wyllene have one son, Steve and five grandchildren.

Wyllene accepted Christ at the age of 8 at St. Paul Methodist A.M.E. Church in Montgomery, Al. Her church history includes St. Mark Presbyterian, St. Paul UMC and presently Aldersgate UMC all located in Cleveland.

Education: B.S degree from Alabama State University, Montgomery, Al., MA degree from Case Western Reserve University, Cleveland, Ohio. Post graduate work, John Carroll University and Cleveland State University, Cleveland, Ohio for certification in Administration and Supervision.

Career: 6th grade teacher, Math Consultant, Administrative Intern, Reading Consultant. She is now retired.

Wyllene has always been involved in church. She has served as Vice President of local UMW. Sunday School Superintendent and Sunday School Teacher. Director of Christian Education, Member and Chairman of Courtesy Committee, Secretary of District UMW.

Chairman of Christian Personhood for Conference UMW She is a member of the District Communications Committee and a writer for Cleveland Together, District newsletter, recently renamed North Coast Crossings. She is a member of the Communication Committee and a writer for the Beacon, Aldersgate newsletter. She has served as Lay Leader for Aldersgate. She is a certified Lay Speaker. Wyllene is a member of the Stewardship Committee and sings with the Vision Choir. She is Co-Chairman of the Shepherd Ministry. She works with Vacation Bible School.

Wyllene helped to establish Reading Enrichment for Adult Development (READ) in 1984, an agency to help adults learn to read and to eradicate illiteracy. She conducts Tutor Training Workshops. She is an active member of the Board of Directors and Chairman of the Benevolent Committee.

Wyllene is a life member of Alpha Kappa Alpha Sorority, Incorporated and has held many positions in her chapter including president.

She is a faithful Christian, a loving wife, a caring mother and grandmother, a dependable friend.

One of Wyllene's favorite verses: Psalm 27:1 The Lord is my light and my salvation- so why should I be afraid?

*SPECIAL TRIBUTES
TO WYLLENE B. WALL*

My dear cousin, is now, and always has been a great inspiration to me. Who is better qualified to pass on words of wisdom?

From humble birth, in a southern city, reared by only a father, she has chartered her course alone. She has always been an avid reader and a bright scholar. Through trial and error, she has made it to this point, gaining wisdom, which she now imparts to me, and all who will listen.

She is also a collector of tidbits of wisdom from other sources. She happily passes them along to you. Read these poems with a desire to replicate her journey on this path.

Mary A. Jackson

****

I consider my self as fortunate to have had you for a dear friend for so many years. You have been closer than a sister to me. My sincere best wishes as you publish "Words of Wisdom," I am so proud of you

Yvonne Gooch

What a unique personality! One that is filled with fun and unusual expressions. Working with her on several committees was an experience. Wyllene always had something funny to say. She is one who could laugh at herself.

She is a wonderful sisterly soror.

Georgette Wood (Gigi)
Lambda Phi Omega Chapter

****

I am very enthusiastic about this opportunity to say something about my friend Wyllene Wall. She is someone whom I admire for several reasons.

Wyllene and I first met over twenty years ago as members of the Alpha Kappa Alpha Sorority. She was and still is utterly devoted to the goals of our sorority. She has shown her devotion to our causes by working tirelessly on the projects that make our community a better place. There is something inside of Wyllene that compels her to do her best for others.

As a Cleveland Public School teacher, Wyllene was the consummate professional educator. Years ago one of her students was Claudia Booker. Today, Claudia is a prominent attorney in Washington, D.C. After all of these years, Claudia's mother insists that having Wyllene for a teacher was a life altering experience for her daughter. Claudia's mother said of her, "My daughter was just an ordinary little girl going to school. Then she was placed in Wyllene's class in the third grade. There, she was transformed into a student with intellectual interests and a huge commitment to her own intellectual development." Wyllene has inspired Claudia and hundreds of other students to do their best.

Both her service to Alpha Kappa Alpha and her public school career are remarkable. But they pale when they are compared to her most outstanding trait- the goodness of her soul. I have never met anyone who does a better job of making Christian principles come alive in her everyday life.

Whenever I see Wyllene I am reminded of the fifth chapter of Galatians, the twenty second verse. "But the fruits of the Spirit are love, joy, peace, long suffering, kindness, goodness, faithfulness, gentleness and self-control." Wyllene exhibits an unshakable joy, regardless of circumstances, and possesses an inner peace which encourages others. She knows how to wait patiently for the results of her labor as she is faithful to the mission. Her kindness and gentleness control her inner strength, so that she knows how to be both tough and tender. Her actions are motivated by the desire to love and serve mankind. She wants the best for others and does her part to see that they get it.

Gail Rose
President Lambda Phi Omega Chapter 1986-1987

Wyllene,

W   Wordsmith extraordinaire
Y   Young at heart, Yummy
L   Loyal to friends
L   Loving to family
E   Energetic, Enthusiastic, Effervescent
N   Never at a loss for words of wisdom
E   Eye-poppingly unforgettable

I have been imprinted by your zest for the best.

Mildred Gardner
President Lambda Phi Omega Chapter 1988-1991

****

Over the years, I have known Wyllene to have a *"Love Affair"* with words. Prose, poetry, and written commentary is part of her very being- how she sees nature, the seasons of the year, the minute things surrounding us which might be overlooked by some. Her words are used to affirm, command, counsel, identify and explore; to worship, reflect, praise and surrender. Mostly they are used to transcend one to a deeper place to reflect and validate.

Congratulation on putting them all together in your book!

Lilloise Talley
President Lambda Phi Omega Chapter 1992-1993

****

I have known Wyllene Wall all of my life. She and my parents were friends before I was born. Although she is not the reason I became a member of Alpha Kappa Alpha Sorority, Inc., she is the reason that I am currently active and a member of Lambda Phi Omega Chapter. Wyllene stayed on my case once she found out that I was an AKA and had moved back to Cleveland.

It was not until I got to know her/within the sorority that I realized how sweet and talented she was. She is a gracious hostess and a generous person. She always sees the good and understands the need to make lemonade when she is handed lemons. All of my previous experiences had been as a child in the company of adults. Besides, I would visit her to see her stepdaughter.

As an adult, I paid attention to her ability to try to keep peace and harmony. Who knew Wyllene was such a talented writer. Her ability to write poems is fantastic. She can take any subject or occasion and write words that roll off of one's tongue like velvet or silk.

Having studied leaders and observing how those they lead react, I took notes on what worked and tried not to repeat what didn't. Of course I am my own person but during my tenure as basileus (president), I always encouraged sisterliness and tried to alleviate cliques and negativity. Wyllene was partially my inspiration.

When I decided to run for basileus, Soror Wyllene strongly discouraged me because of the demand on one's time and because I had a young child. She even spoke with my mother to get her to reason with me. However, at that point I had achieved all of the success at the chapter level that I wanted except basileus. I felt someone younger needed to step up to the plate. After I became basileus, Wyllene was supportive and provided me with encouragement.

With the challenges of my administration, I would say being basileus brought home the need for diplomacy, being prepared, knowledgeable about documents and pertinent subjects, tact and the ability to remain cool and personable in the face of negativity and personal attacks.

Soror Wyllene I thank you for insisting that I reactivate. I would have missed meeting so many wonderful women and missed to many opportunities. Most of all I would probably not gotten to know how talented you are.

Harriet Niles
President Lambda Phi Omega Chapter 1994-1997

****

Wyllene Wall, always a lady, a friend, a soror...gracious, kind and helpful who will always be admired, emulated and cherished by not only me but many.

Cheryl Broussard
President Lambda Phi Omega Chapter 1998-2001

****

I have known soror Wyllene Wall for many years. Throughout our friendship, I have found her to be a:

W	Willing servant to God and all mankind
Y	Youth-oriented teacher and grandmother
L	Loyal friend, sister and Soror
L	Loveable, caring and kind coworker
E	Enthusiastic supporter
N	Noteworthy poetic and creative writer
E	Exemplar of excellence in everything she does.

These are the many facets of Wyllene Wall. Her many talents and interests provide a rich reservoir of experiences to fuel her writing. I am delighted that she is leaving a legacy of her great work for future generations to enjoy.

Reba Denmark
President Lambda Phi Omega Chapter 2002 – 2005

****

Carry our legacy, Wyllene Wall would say....and in the face of power, opposition and fear, see through to light and root yourselves in clear reality ...be straightened by hope and the belief that you truly can make change come about. Wyllene Wall has shown all women how to be leaning posts and gentle shoulders to depend upon. Thank you for such a wonderful spirit.

With much love,

Joyce L. Walker
President, Lambda Phi Omega Chapter 2006-2009

THE WONDERFUL SORORITY OF ALPHA KAPPA ALPHA (AKA)

OUR RATIONALE FOR CHARTERING A NEW CLEVELAND CHAPTER

Soror Madelyn Hairston, Great Lakes Regional Director, Soror Genny Maiden, Soror Geneva B. Maiden, Fellow Greeks, Friends and sorors. We who are gathered here today, on this significant occasion are witnessing or participating in "history in the making."

Today is a "first" for Cleveland, the first chartering of a second graduate chapter of Alpha Kappa Alpha Sorority, Incorporated. Many of you might be curious, even critical concerning the reasons for establishing this new chapter. We would like to share our rationale and at the same time allay any wrong conceptions or incorrect rumors.

First, I would like to say this was not a quick decision. For years, we have been aware of the number and strength of our sorors in Cleveland. We have looked at other cities. Cleveland is one of the few major cities without two graduate chapters. Detroit, Los Angeles, Chicago, New York, Oklahoma City, Jefferson City, Muskogee City, Oklahoma, all have more than one Alumnae chapter. We discovered that these chapters work harmoniously and effectively together and politically were a force to be reckoned with. The talents and leadership skills of more sorors could be utilized. The potential for attracting inactive sorors who preferred a smaller chapter was another factor.

Secondly, we were concerned with the growth of our present chapter, Alpha Omega. with an approximate membership of two hundred eighty sorors presented a housing problem for meetings and for sorors to really get to know each other.

Thirdly, as we studied the effectiveness of various chapters, it was apparent that those with smaller memberships were stronger, more productive, more involved in all chapter activities. We felt a smaller chapter would offer greater opportunities for individual participation in chapter programs and activities. We would be able to tap the potential and talent of many more sorors. A smaller, chapter offers a more intimate sisterhood.

So far we have discussed active sorors. Fourthly, we were concerned for more than three hundred inactive sorors in the greater Cleveland area. Many find it difficult to function in such a large group. A second chapter would meet the needs of these sorors. The establishment of a second graduate chapter is a thrust toward a third chapter. Detroit is in the process of chartering its fourth graduate chapter. Cleveland certainly has the potential in numbers and talent.

Finally, we would like to emphasize that the new chapter will not be in competition with the present chapter. We expect to work on many shared activities. Both chapters would be involved in the same national target goals. We will maintain and foster the same sisterly love for each other and for Alpha Kappa Alpha Sorority, Inc. We will always respect and revere Alpha Omega for being the oldest chapter in Alpha Kappa Alpha Sorority, Incorporated.

LAMBDA PHI OMEGA CHARTERING POEM
March 13, 1978

Another vine is beginning to grow,
Green, strong and true
The nurture of this "Ivy vine"
Depends on each of you.

Each one who shares this honor,
Who signs the charter today,
Is committed to all the ideals
That Alpha Kappa Alpha portrays.

Each leaf on the vine has its purpose,
Although a segment of the greater whole,
So each soror has a part,
Playing her special role.

In sisterly love let's band together,
Our dreams, goals and hopes,
To make Alpha Kappa Alpha ever better,
And broaden Cleveland's scope.

We, who are being chartered,
Serene, sure, arrayed in white,
Touched forever by Alpha Kappa Alpha's vision
Service to all mankind as we spread the light.

Alpha Kappa Alpha Sorority, Inc.
Rich in heritage, steeped in tradition, continues to grow
Through insight and foresight of sorors we know.
Susie L. Rice, Geneva, B. Maiden, Dorothy Bassett,

Thelma Dockens Georgette Wood, just to name a few,
Dedicated, diligent sorors
Whose loyalty to Alpha Kappa Alpha
No one can ever subdue.

They encountered doubt, criticism,
And all the rest,
But they still continued to do
What they thought was best.

Today, let us clap our hands,
Let us toot our horn,
Because on this day, March 18, 1978
A new Cleveland Chapter is born.

PEARL DAY INTERVIEW GUIDE

Charter Member Name: Soror Wyllene Brown Wall
Interviewer's Name: Soror Willa Walker

a. **Charter Member's role in the formation of Lambda Phi Omega**
I was one of the 25 members, non officer needed to charter another graduate chapter.

b. **Atmosphere that surrounded the formation of Lambda Phi Omega**
Unfortunately there were those who objected, who thought we were making a mistake and actually being disloyal as sorors. I like to believe this number is in the minority. Most sorors have healed and moved on to acceptance and cooperation. After all, we are all Alpha Kappa Alpha Women.

c. **Charter Member's personal reaction to the new formation of Lambda Phi Omega**
Frankly, I was excited about having another chapter. Sorors had a choice. Many cities had two chapters and so we like New York, Detroit, Los Angeles, New Orleans had more then two. Cleveland was just beginning to take some action. I would feel the same way should a group of sorors feel the need for a third graduate chapter. As an undergraduate I was a member of a small close knit chapter and when I joined Alpha Omega I missed this close bond of sisterhood.

d. **Positive Outcomes before and after the formation of Lambda Phi Omega**
It wasn't difficult to find 25 active sorors who responded to the letter that was mailed. We were chartered with 71 members, March 18, 1978. Soror Madelyn Hairston –

Giddings was the Great Lakes Regional Director and Soror Bernice I Sumlin was Supreme Basileus. Officers were elected. The Inter Chapter Relations Committee was formed with equal members from each chapter to establish guidelines in areas in which we planned to work together. The Boule' was held in Houston Texas in 1978 and Lambda Phi Omega attended its first Boule. Our belated, first Basileus Geneva B. Maiden knitted a rug which was raffled off at the Boule'.

e. **Cleveland's reaction to the existence of two chapters of Alpha Kappa Alpha Sorority, Incorporated.**
All Greek letter sororities and fraternities were invited to the chartering held at the Holiday Inn, then located on the corner of Emery and Northfield Road 21 years ago. They congratulated the "New Star in the Galaxy." The citizens of Cleveland have accepted and give support to both chapters.

f. **Other Comments**
I love and respect all sorors of both chapters because I believe we are working to perpetuate Alpha Kappa Alpha Sorority, Incorporated the principals and programs which make it an organization which is supreme in service to all mankind. "So _together_ anew we will pledge our faith, and _united_ we'll forge away."

THE LIVING BLOOD-SACRIFICIAL GIVING

Gal. 6:2
"Bear ye one another's burdens, and so fulfill the law of Christ."

Matt: 5:16
"Let your light shine before men, that they may see your good deeds and praise your Father in heaven."

When I reflect on the living blood, I immediately think of how Jesus gave his life to save the world from sin. Again, I am reminded how Jesus asked us to remember this during Communion. The Hymnist, Robert Lowry, wrote, "What can wash away my sins? Nothing but the blood of Jesus." "What can make me whole again? Nothing but the blood of Jesus."

Another Hymnist, Andrae Crouch, sings "The blood that gives me strength from day to day- it will never lose its power."

Just recently, Alpha Kappa Alpha Sorority, Incorporated worked with the American Red Cross during their blood drive. The Health Chairman, Sarah Britton and her committee worked hard to increase the number of blood donors but it soon became apparent that the percentage of donors has decreased. One of the primary reasons is fear. Giving blood is completely safe. It is impossible to contract AIDS by giving blood. A new needle is used for one donor and one donor only. After it is used, it is destroyed. Your blood donation will bring you the satisfaction of helping others in need. Many patients need blood to survive.

Sarah and her committee also held several bone marrow donor drives. They distributed educational material about procedures targeting the African American community where donors are especially needed with little success. The demand is crucial and growing. The mother, who decided to have a baby so that its bone marrow could be used to save her critically ill daughter is an example of the long wait to get the perfect match. Your bone marrow could save somebody's life.

I interviewed a mother, Mrs. Ridgely Worthy, whose son, Brandon, born June 2, 1980 was diagnosed at six years of age with, Aplastic Anemenia Fanconi, the worst kind. The only cure was a bone marrow transplant.

Unfortunately, neither the parents or siblings were good matches. Testing was extended to other family members with no success. Therefore, Brandon's name was placed on the National Bone Marrow Bank and the long wait began. In the mean time, Brandon was kept alive with frequently blood transfusions.

As a terminally ill child, Brandon was granted his dearest wish, a trip to Los Angeles to see Arsenio Hall in October 1989. He was so happy and thrilled.

By the end of October, a donor was found, not a perfect match but close enough to give Brandon a chance to live. Mother, father and Brandon went to Iowa where they were to stay four months. The parents lived in Ronald McDonald House at $1.00 per night. Mrs. Worthy could not praise this facility enough; the volunteers were wonderful. They supplied food, beverages and loving moral support. While there, she witnessed the death of 14 children.

The cost of the transplant was exorbitant, about a half million dollars. Good insurance paid most of it.

Brandon was given massive doses of chemotherapy. His school work continued, his teacher in Beachwood sent his homework, letters and boxes of things from his classmates. They also sent flowers but they were not allowed. His teacher and classmates raised $12,000 to help. Ms. Worthy said she can't ever forget the care and support she and her family received, or thank them enough.

The long wait for a donor and the chemo treatments took its toll on Brandon. The chemo destroyed his immune system. His donor was an unrelated white female. Brandon died from renal failure, February 15, 1990.

L.T.V. Steel, where Mr. Worthy worked, wrote a book entitled, "Brandon," compiled from the reports they had received from Mr. Worthy almost daily.

Mrs. Worthy and her family are advocates for bone marrow donors. While it is possible for an African American patient to match a donor from any race or ethnic group, the most likely bone marrow is from an African American donor.

THE HISTORY OF JOB CORP
JEWEL OF AN IDEA

The vision and foresight of Alpha Kappa Alpha Women recognize no limit in fostering their aim of "Service to all mankind."

To render a service to those in need,
Is an ultimate effort indeed.

To youth who have lost their way,
To help them see a better way.

Dormant dreamer awaken,
Wasteful lives forsaken.

This was the dream in the minds
O the sorors who wrote the lines.

For the proposal to Cleveland to begin a venture,
Known as The Job Corp Center.

In 1964 President Johnson signed the Economic Opportunity Act
Our sorority, through its Program Committee did react.

The proposal which was written by the office of Economic Opportunity
Was the combined effort of Alpha Kappa Alpha women:
Mary Chambers, Bernice Sumlin, Carey B. Preston, Carrie Belle Cooke,
Dr. Rose Butler-Brown, Abigail Hobson, Willhelmenia B. Drake, Flossie Diamond, Ethel
James Williams, Dr. Eleanor Ison Franklin, Esther Pollard and Supreme Basileus, Julia Purnell

These Sorors solved a dilemma!

Mary Chambers, First Director of the Center
Was there to help those who would enter.

The success of the Center was due to her labors,
Her eye for details, a distinctive favor.

The first site on Ansel Road
Consisted of three dormitory floors.

Eighty seven and five percent is the average rate of employment,
This achievement gives to many great courage and enjoyment.

CLEVELAND JOB CORP CENTER

In 1973 the Job Corp Center was moved to its present location on Carnegie Avenue.
The entire building when renovated served very well as contemplated.

Instead, non resident women and men,
Were included in the new trend.

Some Centers were reduced in size or closed,
Fortunately, we were not one of those.

Placement and financing of jobs for Corps graduates was a priority,
92 percent placement was accomplished by Alpha Kappa Alpha Sorority.

An agreement with Brotherhood of Railing and Airlines was significant,
It turned out to be magnificent.

The first woman plasterer, sheet metal worker and brakeman were placed,
This occurred during the Center's first phase.

J	Jewel of an idea
O	Opportunity Act
B	Best Proposal
C	Chambers, Mary First Job Corp Center Director
O	On Carnegie Ave
R	Its new relocation
P	Placement of students
S	Self esteem

C	Contract, full responsibility
E	Eligibility of enrollees
N	Notable Directors, Sorors, Zelma George and Jean Ward Walker
T	Training
E	Enriching experiences
R	Self Esteem

Self esteem grows through work, for which enrollees are trained,
Failures and mistakes are forgotten and so is the pain.

A Purposeful attitude and a positive goal,
Started at the center and developed into a life long role.

Contract: Full responsibility

In 1968, Alpha Kappa Alpha Sorority became the sole contractor,
Including fiscal, administrative, and other factors.

The Zelma George Incentive Fund;

Contributions from Alpha Kappa Chapters,
Incentive awards and sisterly rapture.

ELEGIBILITY:

Any young woman, unemployed, out of school, sixteen to twenty one,
Free from mental and physical defects is welcome to come.

Applicants are screened by: Women in community on the local level
Final selection is made by Job Corp Center, Federal level.

Dr. Zelma George, versatile, experienced, dynamic and warm,
Used her expertise to inspire the girls to achieve and perform.

In her leadership, the enrollees were involved,
In enriching experiences and problems were solved.

In 1974, Dr. George retired,
Mrs. Jean Ward Walker was appointed with pride.

Having worked at the Center for nine years,
She approached the task without any fears.

She widened the horizons, changed life style,
Of many men and women by going the extra mile.

Students receive training in all educational courses, music and arts,
Vocational training is also a vital and interesting part.

One year of training, no more than two,
Then the graduates are ready to start anew.

Counseling and guidance helped the student select,
In which vocational area she excels the best.

Students learn to cope in others ways,
Enacting with others, self government, and artistic plays.

Incentive awards were perceived,
For all students who achieved.

Recruitment is now a National target,
Involving all local chapters.

To keep the chapter Center live and thriving,
New enrollees must keep arriving.

ALPHA KAPPA ALPHA SORORITY, INCORPORATED FOUNDERS' DAY

The Cleveland Chapters of AKA: Alpha Omega, Lambda Phi Omega and Omega, had as their theme, "Continuing the Legacy" as they jointly celebrated the founders who established Alpha Kappa Alpha Sorority Incorporated in 1908 at Howard University. Ethel Hedgeman Lyle was the founding spirit of a dream that continues today. The members dressed in pink or green filled to capacity The Manor Party Room, January 31, 1999. Greetings: were extended by the presidents of the chapters: Mrs. Frances Tyus, Mrs. Cheryl Broussard and Ms. Coleen Sullivan for Ms. Michele Hairston. Invocation: Mrs. Martha Eulinberg. Music was furnished by Alpha Kappa Alpha Chorale, Director Tillie Colter. A poem, "How I Feel About Alpha Kappa Alpha Sorority," written and recited by Ms. Lia Richardson, was one of the highlights

Ms. Angela Rush introduced the keynote speaker, Dr. Pamela Redden, immediate, past President of Alpha Omega, and Cluster Coordinator of North Ohio Western PA. She challenged the members to honor the past, to cherish the dream of the founders. She said we must treasure the Legacy left to us; we must preserve it, add to it by increasing its value and pass it on to others.

Ms. Ruth Fore and Mrs. Deborah Dickinson explained what is happening at Triumph House. A donation of $1000 was given to Triumph House. Dr, Marjorie Parker, 15th International President and author "To cherish the past is to enrich today and to strengthen tomorrow."

The Founders' Day Committee: Co-chairs, Angela Rush and Cynthia Spencer; Erma Albriton, Charita Buchanan, Monica Carter, Kim Dashield – Hill, Lori Durham, Carolyn Grimes, Darinka Hardy, Renee Howard, Claudia Ivy – Jackson, Kim

Jackson, Traci James, Marion Johnson, Diana Jones, Tonisha Long, Portia Morgan, Beverly Murphy, Alice Rush, Alma Tanner, Joyce Thornton, Ruth Wesby, Carolyn Wynn.

The program concluded with a Rededication Service.

LAMBDA PHI OMEGA MIP WEEKEND
February 21, 2003

Inspirational Thoughts

Good morning sorors and candidates. I feel very honored to have been asked to give five minutes of inspirational thoughts. I am reminded of a little boy who stood in church gazing at a plaque with a puzzled expression on his face. The pastor walked over and spoke to him and told him the names on the plaque were those who died in service. The little boy began to tremble and the pastor concerned asked what was wrong. The little boy asked was it the 8:45 service or the 10:45 service?

Scripture: 1 Cor. 2:9 What no eye has seen, nor ear heard, nor the heart of man conceived, what God has prepared for those who love him.

Let us pray: Father, we thank you for the sorors assembled here today and for the candidates who wish to unite with us. May all that we do today be pleasing in your sight and receive your blessing. Amen.

The Membership Intake Process, even in its present abbreviated form is an exciting time not only for the candidates but its excitement includes all of us, 1st year sorors through Silver, Golden and Diamond sorors. MIP offers an opportunity for us to evaluate and assess our commitment and dedication to Alpha Kappa Alpha Sorority, Incorporated on a personal level. It is a time when we pledge anew our love and loyalty as we prepare to welcome our new members into our sisterhood.

Please repeat after me: Dear God, make me a channel through which your blessings flow.

Today soror, is our day to share, to bless to uplift, to enrich our world. If there is a word we can lovingly speak, if there is a loving action we can take, we should speak that word and take that action.

We should be open to ways that we can help to make life happier and better, not just for ourselves but for others. Even as we see a need, we should also see a way that the need can be fulfilled.

To highlight one of our founders, Norma Elizabeth Boyd was such a channel. She worked tirelessly for racial justice and for children's rights. The benefits from her autobiographical book, "A love that Equals My Labors," will go for the children's projects sponsored by Alpha Kappa Alpha Sorority, Incorporated and to the Women's International Religious Fellowship. I highly recommend the reading of Soror Boyd's book.

I close with this slogan by John Wesley. "Do all the good you can, in all the places you can to every person you can in every way you can for as long as you can. In the name of Jesus we pray. Amen

LAMBDA PHI OMEGA CHAPTER
ALPHA KAPPA ALPHA SORORITY, INCORPORATED

Welcome to our glorious sisterhood.

I look forward to seeing you very soon. Until then enjoy and learn about our chapter and sorority.

Think about what you want to do as a member of our chapter.

God loves you and so do I.

A WELCOME TO NEW SORORS

Today, you have become an Alpha Kappa Alpha Woman. You have taken a vow and joined over 75,000 "Sorors Strong." From this moment, you will begin your life as an Alpha Kappa Alpha Woman. I hope it will mean as much to you twenty years hence as it does at this point in time. I would like to leave you with this recipe for becoming a true soror. It is called:

SOROR "BRED"

Take three or more National Targets. Stir them one at a time in a large mixing bowl, making sure that each ingredient receives the same number of beats. Next, add an unlimited amount of Time, Patience and Stamina to the mixture, beat well until smooth and consistent. Now you are ready to add an unmeasured amount of Knowledge and Creativity, blend carefully so you don't ruffle the smooth texture. Flavor generously with a large quantity of Love and Devotion. Let rise indefinitely in a warm, congenial temperature of Meetings, Clusters, Regional Conferences and Boules. Finally, bake in a hot oven of Sisterly Unity until well done. Set your timer for a lifetime. It takes that long, but the result is well worth the effort.

THE HISTORY OF PEARL DAY

In 1979, Lambda Phi Omega Chapter planned its first Pearl Day, to celebrate chartering achievements and sisterhood in every way.

Soror Thelma Dockens gave Pearl Day its name.

Soror Wyllene gave us our aim: Purposeful, Effective, Annual Reclaim, Retain Luncheon Day. Let us look at other adjectives that could apply: Revive, Reenergize, Renew, Rejuvenate, Revitalize, Reactivate, Yes! Reactivate! Reactivate!

Our apparel would be pink /and or green
Appropriate for the Alpha Kappa Alpha scene.

Our choir, "The Pearls" is beholden,
For its name to Soror Janet Bolden.

The Pearl Day Hymn gives us pleasure
Its author, the late Dorothy Bassett,
Whom we will always treasure.

To our Charter Members, we owe a debt,
Your names are engraved on a plaque less we forget.

Those who are present, please stand now,
Let us see you turn around and take a bow.

One Charter member, Susie L. Rice,
Plans our exhibits which are so nice.

Take a few minutes to view the history.
So that Lambda Phi Omega will not be a mystery.

The years of celebration have included
Speakers, Pep Songs and skits galore,
Sorors always have something exciting in store.

PEARL DAY
HILTON EAST
March 29, 2008,

Distinguished Sorors on the dais, visiting, sorors, inactive sorors, sorors of Lambda Phi Omega Chapter, Alpha Kappa Sorority, Incorporated, Good Afternoon.

As I look around, I see a beautiful group of Alpha Kappa women dressed in pink or green. You create a beautiful scene; pink and green everywhere dominate this setting and unites us in unity and sisterhood.

It is my pleasure to present a first time award to the Outstanding Soror of Lambda Phi Omega Chapter of Alpha Kappa Alpha Sorority for 2006. The criteria for this award will be published in "The Vine." Will the Winner, Soror Doris Holland Olukoya please come forward.

The next award is for a new Golden Soror 2008, Soror Mildred Brown Gardner. Would you please come forward. I am delighted to present you with this award on becoming a Golden Soror.

25ᵀᴴ PEARL DAY
EMBASSY SUITES
March 28, 2003

Theme: 25 years perpetuating the spirit of Alpha Kappa Alpha Sorority, Incorporated.

Introduction of soror Madelyn Hairston Giddens by Soror Wyllene B. Wall.

This is an appropriate time to introduce the person who chartered Lambda Phi Omega Chapter in 1978, Soror Madelyn Hairston Giddens. 17th Great Lakes Regional Director 1974 - 1978.

Education: Bachelor of Science Major in English and History, Miner Teachers College, Washington D.C. Class of 1946. Master of Secondary Education, University of Pittsburgh. 1958, Reading Specialist, Secondary Principal Certification, Further study University of South Carolina and Bank Street University, New York.

Soror Madelyn served as Basileus of her chapter, Alpha Alpha Omega, located in Pittsburgh, PA. 1972 - 1973. She also served as Hodegos. She has actually chaired all committees in Alpha Alpha Omega during her years as a member. Presently, she is chairman of Ways and Means Committee.

On the Regional Level she has chaired, Time and Place, Regional Awards, Job Corps, Standards and Election Committees.

Soror Madelyn served 4 years on the International Committee of Silver Stars, Golden Sorors and Diamond Stars.

Soror Madelyn has conducted a variety of workshops on the Local, Regional and National levels of Alpha Kappa Alpha Sorority, Incorporated.

She is a member of St. James A.M.E. Church where she is busy with the National Advisory Committee and Trustee Board. She assisted the "Need" Board in raising over a million dollars for scholarships.

Please help me welcome Soror Madelyn Hairston Giddens, 17th Great Lakes Regional Director.

PEARL DAY
MEDITERRANEAN PARTY CENTER
March 23, 2002 11:30 A.M.

To Soror Reba Denmark, Basileus, Soror Dolores Best, Chairman and Soror Gloria Glover, Co-Chairman and to all sorors who love and serve Alpha Kappa Alpha Sorority, Incorporated, Good afternoon.

Today we celebrate our 24th Pearl Day with the theme, "Uniting Sisterhood Through Spirituality." What is spirituality? Yours, mine and ours. I like to think of spirituality as a personal relationship with God. It begins with love, God's love for us, so great that he gave his only son to save the world. Jesus Christ, the Son of God instructs us to love our neighbor as we love our self.

Another key word is commitment. Again, God placed the care of the Universe in the hands of man. We are responsible to protect the inhabitants of the earth and preservation of the natural resources of the world. Love and commitment are the barometers that test our spirituality.

I leave these final thoughts with you in regard to your spirituality in your chapter:

> *Sorors accept our spiritual life*
> *With joy, love and songs,*
> *Embrace our spiritual life*
> *With the desire to right all wrongs.*
>
> *Sorors, demonstrate our spiritual life*
> *With pride and respect for each other,*
> *Strengthen our legacy through family*
> *You are blessed through, sister, aunt,*
> *grandmother or mother.*

Sorors believe in our spiritual life.
Commit to our programs this year,
United, committed with spirituality
To all that we hold dear.

GETTING READY FOR SORORITY MEETING
August 7, 2001

Soror _____ is talking on her cell phone to see if Soror _____ is home.

1st S "Hi _____ I want to stop by for a short visit if you are not busy."

2nd S "I'm never too busy to see you, so glad you are on your way."

2nd S (Keeps busy tiding the room and humming s song until the doorbell rings.)

2nd S "Hi Soror _____" (they exchange sisterly hugs and greetings) "Come on in."

1st S "Gee, this is a busy weekend! What are you wearing to the Jazz Concert tonight?"

2nd S "I'm not telling. I plan to surprise you."

1st S "Remember we have Sorority Meeting tomorrow morning. What does an Alpha Kappa Woman exemplify at all times?"

2nd S "Well she has poise which means composure, polish which means refinement and pizzazz meaning flare which I have in abundance" (she says as she walks over to the table to get her sorority bag) "What is this document?"

1st S "It's the Constitution, (she names the next two documents as 2nd S takes them from her bag) the Manual of Standard Procedures, the Bylaws of Lambda Phi Omega. Each soror should bring these three documents to Executive Meetings, General Meetings, workshops,

Retreats, Clusters, Regionals and Boules. What else is in your bag soror _____?" (she asks with a laugh)?

2ⁿᵈ S "Each soror with poise, polish and pizzazz should own a copy of the following: Robert's Rules of Order, Graduate Membership Intake Process (MIP), Protocol, So Now You are Elected, "Alpha Kappa Alpha "In the Eye of the Beholder," by Marjorie H. Parker and "A Love That Equals My Labors," by Norma E. Boyd and a Roster of the members. It would be great to have a pictorial roster!"

1ˢᵗ S "All Lambda Phi Omega sorors have poise, polish and pizzazz! That's a good idea, a Pictorial Directory." (she says taking her leave) "Bye see you Saturday."

Written by Sorors: Wyllene B. Wall and Georgette Wood (Gigi)

LAMBDA PHI OMEGA CHAPTER
CELEBRATES 10TH AUTUMN AFFAIR

The elegant, gracious atmosphere of the Manor Party Center was the setting for almost 500 guests who set the tone for a Sophisticated Soiree. The members and their guests were beautifully attired for the evening greeting old friends and meeting new ones

The President, Joyce Walker and The Ways and Means Committee, Chairman, Wyllene Wall are grateful to all who came to make this our 10th fund raising for scholarships which benefit deserving students in Cleveland and surrounding areas an overwhelming success.

As usual, the variety of Hors d'oeuvres were abundant and delicious. The Benjamins Band was scintillating and the vocalist's rendition of popular songs captivated the crowd. Dee Jay Ralph selections kept the dance floor full with choices for young, old and in between.

There were many exciting surprises: Mr. and Mrs. Larry Gates from Akron performed "Detroit Style Ball Rooming." Door prizes were given to 5 winners. Each guest received The 10th Anniversary Souvenir Booklet. Each person also received the gift of A Weekly Pocket Planner for 2007, compliments of Great Lakes Physicians. Lastly there was the Cash Raffle.

During intermission, The Chairman, Wyllene Wall thanked the audience and introduced the members of the Ways and Means Committee. Joyce Walker, President also expressed gratitude for the supporters and introduced the corporate sponsors. The AKA'S sang the National Hymn led by Elizabeth Jones. After intermission, the crowd danced and danced.

LAMBDA PHI OMEGA CHAPTER
STRATEGIC PLANNING COMMITTEE
MAPLE HEIGHTS LIBRARY
October 18, 2003- 9:30 A.M.

The question posed for each committee to bring to this session, what project do you think would make the greatest long-term impact on the community? What dream do we have that would make a difference in our chapter and in the community. I thought about this, I prayed about this. The Ways and Means Committee has not met since the last chapter meeting, which took place at the Retreat so we haven't had a discussion. However, I have always had a dream of this chapter, my chapter, acquiring an AKA house. I envision this house as a place to:

- Hold chapter meetings
- Committee meetings
- Store all chapter equipment and documents
- A center for tutoring children
- A center for senior citizens
- Rooms for housing visiting sorors
- Rent meeting rooms to other organizations
- A place to display chapter awards and trophy's
- Furnish an office with all the latest equipment

The Housing Committee, The Economic Development Committee and Ways and Means Committee would work in collaboration on this project. I believe that we could make this dream a reality in 5 years. For instance if each soror would contribute $100.00 a year we would generate $10,000 with a membership of 100 members. The committees would also explore other means of adding to the housing fund.

Sorors, I hope you can dream with me in owning our AKA HOUSE. *Soror Wyllene Wall chairman Ways and Means.*

MY SPECIAL AKA POEMS

LET'S BE TRUE TO OUR COLORS

Let us return to our true colors,
Salmon pink and apple green.

Let's not compromise with shocking pink,
You wouldn't settle for fake fur instead of mink!

Let us not settle for rose or mauve,
That's not the color to be AKA suave.

Fuchsia, some sorors have worn,
Now that's an AKA thorn

Fuchsia is a shade of red,
Nothing more needs to be said!

There are all shades of green,
That I've seen make the AKA scene.

Look at lime or chartreuse,
Neither is suitable for AKA use.

Kelly green is pretty and bright,
On AKA's have been an acceptable sight

Kelly green is not the color our Founders wore,
Apple green is the preferred shade at any store.

Our color is not avocado, emerald or jade,
Although either color is a beautiful shade.

Some of us have even accepted turquoise or moss,
Any green is up for a toss.

Are we becoming color blind?
Is the external acceptance of any shade of pink and green
indicative of an internal weakening of the principles and
traditions of Alpha Kappa Alpha Sorority?

Our sorors are wearing pink and green,
and every shade in between.

Sorors let us return to our true colors,
Salmon Pink and Apple Green.

ALPHA KAPPA ALPHA SORORITY, INCORPORATED
"FASHIONETTA"
1966

F	With fascinating flamboyant fashions that flatter the feminine form
A	Admire the alluring attire, appropriate accessories accenting the aesthetic and filling your Adonis with admiration.
S	See the sensational, scintillating, spectacular styles.
H	High lightening hobby and home.
I	Inspect the imaginative, individualistic apparel.
O	Observe the originals of great designers.
N	Note the numerous novel raiments.
E	Easily the epitome of elegance.
T	Taking this tantalizing, tempting array of
T	Thrilling transcendent fashions
A	Alpha Kappa Alpha presents its "Summer Scene."
F	Fashionable Fashionetta
I	Intended to inspire and impress you.
N	Naturally, nothing has been neglected.
A	Admirable audience, "adieu."
L	Lovely, Lads and Ladies when you leave you
E	End an enchanted evening of ecstatic elegance.

A CHORAL READING FOR IVIES

We were proud Ivies,
Wearing Salmon pink and apple green.
We cherished the Alpha Kappa Alpha dream.

We were the first Ivies made,
Part of history that will never fade...

Sincere in our vows, loyal and true,
Service to mankind unselfish and pure.

The first to "Capture a vision fair"
To share a life time of sisterhood rare!

OUR SPIRITUAL LIFE

Sorors, accept our spiritual life
With joy, love and songs,
Embrace our spiritual life
With the desire to right all wrongs.

Sorors, demonstrate our spiritual life
With pride and respect for each other,
Strengthen our legacy through family
If you are a mother or grandmother.

Sorors, believe in our spiritual life,
Commit to our programs this year.
Spread our spirituality and love,
To all whom we hold dear.

AN AKA PRAYER

Show me Dear Lord, your loving way,
With twenty pearls on my heart, I humbly pray.

For my sisters who are both far and near,
Thank you Dear Lord for all the past years.

For a sisterhood that is so profound,
Since 1908, with ivy always around.

Lambda Phi Omega Chapter also was found,
The decision by the group has proven sound.

For thirty one years we have grown,
Throughout the region we are known.

With your gracious guidance, our faith soars;
With your wisdom our enthusiasm roars,

To serve you, to praise you is our sisterly task,
Only your steadfast strength can keep us steadfast.

In your bountiful way,
Bless all who are present,
And those who are absent today
And Lord bless AKA!

ALL SOROR SAY, "AMEN."

SOMEWHERE OUT THERE
February 13, 1989

SOMEWHERE OUT THERE, sorors shine a bright light,
Sorors are thinking of you and loving you tonight.

SOMEWHERE OUT THERE you are saying a prayer,
That we'll find our Zodiac in that Big Somewhere Out There.

Even though we know how very different we are,
It helps to think Lambda Phi Omega is our bright star.

And our star signs, Aries to Pisces meld a perfect lullaby.
It helps to think we're harmonizing under the same sky.

SOMEWHERE OUT THERE, if, AKA can see us through,
Then we'll be sorors, Somewhere Out There, where dreams come true.

And love will see us through, then we'll be sorors
Somewhere Out There, where dreams come true.

A PANTRY SHOWER

A bridal shower is always enticing,
An affair like this can be most exciting
A "Pantry Shower" is the theme,
Let us begin with our scheme,
To fill the larder with lots of staples,
So _____ can cook when she reads the labels.
Sugar is a must you know,
To sweeten things and make love grow.
Grits are food for the soul,
Morning when the weather is cold.
Flour for breads is a must,
Cakes, cookies, and flaky crusts.
There are mixes and mixes galore,
Just look on the shelf of any food store.
Herbs, exotic and rare,
Become a gourmet cook with a special flare.
Spices give food just the right zest,
Enhancing aroma, flavoring food the best.
Canned foods are quick and easy to use,
No way can they a novice confuse.
Coffee, cocoa and a variety of teas,
Small and large cans of tasty peas.
Rice can be prepared any way you wish,
It always makes a tempting dish.
Use canned fruits when fresh fruit is not in season
Yet, there might be many other reasons.
Dried fruits can be kept on the shelf,
To use when no fresh fruit is left.
Noodles come in all sizes and shapes,
For cheese and other casserole bakes.
Join the "Pantry Shower" for Soror _____,
Your category is _____.

HOME COMING TEA

Good afternoon my dear sorors, you are lovely all dressed for tea! Today let us rejoice, enjoy and be carefree on this day that the Lord has made. Let us capture the "Spirit of AKA. For some of us it will be recapturing.

S   Sisterhood warm, and rare,
       An emotion all sorors share.

P   Programs of service to all mankind,
       The American Red Cross and Pims come to mind.

I   Involvement at the Local, Regional and International levels.

R   Reclaiming, Retaining, sorors would be like heaven.
       Renewal, reenergizing, and vitalizing of self,
       Keeps you busy as a sisterly elf.

I   Inspiration from without and within,
       With this we are sure to win.

T   Technology is with us and we must learn,
       Technological mysteries to discern.

O   Outstanding, Outgoing Programs of Care,
F   For all sorors to learn about and be aware.

A   Alpha
K   Kappa
A   Alpha

A RETIREMENT SONNET
Dedicated to Reba Denmark
August 16, 1996

Retirement life is waiting for you,
A time to explore, meet challenges anew,
A time to follow your dreams,
Or invest in business schemes.
Now, you can decide what to do each day,
Whether to clean the house, read a book or play,
Maybe you'll join a shopping tour,
Visiting the children is sure to be another allure.
What ever, it's up to you to decide,
Put all thoughts of substituting aside,
Spend quality time with Dave, alone,
Just relax and enjoy your lovely home.
Wishing you happiness, leisure and health,
More satisfying than any wealth.

AKA HONORS & ACHIEVEMENTS

NOW AND FOREVER
March 2, 2005

Golden Sorors, Golden Sorors Plus, Silver Stars, Silver Stars Plus; and Seasoned Sorors who have been pearls for ten years or more; like to reminisce about yesterdays and the changes that have taken place; under the leadership of each Supreme Basileus as well as under the leadership of each chapter Basileus.

Young and new sorors bring visions and novel innovations. Older sorors are the guardians of our historic past. Proud to share and impart to new sorors sacred traditions that last.

Alpha Kappa Alpha Sorority, Incorporated, is generational in scope. This is how we survive and continue to grow.

What has not changed is the love and commitment that sorors have for Alpha Kappa Alpha Sorority, Incorporated presently, Soror Linda M. White, twenty six Supreme Basileus with her wonderful theme, "The Spirit of Alpha Kappa Alpha Sorority" has been exhilarating.

All sorors play a part
In giving service and continuous help
To all mankind.
In filling a need, we are never slow.
Sorors let us truly love each other.
As God would have us do,
Let us help others and each other.
And respect each other too.

REBA DENMARK BASILEUS OF LAMBDA PHI OMEGA CHAPTER ALPHA KAPPA ALPHA SORORITY, INCORPORATED: 2002-2005
March 27, 2007

R   Resourceful and responsible
E   Extraordinary in all endeavors
B   Believer in the best sisterly behavior
A   Attentive and assertive to all chapter agendas

D   Devoted to demands and details
E   Energetic and enthusiastic in all events
N   Natural narrator and negotiator
M   A mother who started a marvelous legacy. She gave multifaceted service to her church, chapter, community and to all mankind.
A   Admirable as an advisor
R   Respected and respectable
K   Kind and knowledgeable

IN HONOR OF SOROR BARBARA WILLIAMSON

Barbara is a Soror,
Whom we hold very dear,
She is articulate and talented,
Her goals are clear.

She was our chaplain,
Her words of wisdom wrought,
Faithful and caring,
Inspiration she always brought.

She directed the Pearls,
Our new Chorale,
Rehearsing us patiently,
and boostering our morale.

Chairman of Community Relations,
Alert and aware,
Involved in service,
Unselfish and rare.

Barbara is a Soror,
Always in motion,
Busy, but organized,
Whatever the notion.

She has nurtured and used,
Her talents so well,
Her gifts are unique,
As her sorors will tell.

She is the First Anti Basileus,
for Nineteen Eighty two,
We look forward with pleasure,
In working with you.

BARBARA WILLIAMSON

B	is for her Beautiful smile,
A	is for Assuming duties worthwhile,
R	is for Reading which she stresses,
B	is for Benevolence, she addresses,
A	is for her Ardent support of schools,
R	is for her Respect for Rules
A	is Admiration for her teaching tools.
W	is for the Work, she does so well,
I	is for Involvement, nothing can quell.
L	is for Learning all Life Long,
L	is for Loving the Lilt of song.
I	is her Interest for all in need,
A	is for Action with utmost speed.
M	is Mastery of the teaching art,
S	is for Social Studies which she imparts.
O	is for Other dreams to come true,
N	is Never look back, on with the New.

PLAQUE FOR MILDRED BROWN GARDNER

M	Magnificent, Motivator, Mother of three
I	Inspiring, Interesting
L	Loyal, Leader
D	Dedicated, Dignified
R	Religious and Righteous
E	Efficient, Effective
D	Diligent
B	Brilliant
R	Reserved
O	Outspoken
W	Witty
N	Nurturing
G	Generous Golden Soror of 2008
A	Active, Articulate
R	Respected, Respectful
D	Determined, Dutiful
N	Notable Negotiator
E	Earnest, Enlightening
R	Realistic, Responsible

GOLDEN SORORS
2005

G   A golden soror is gentle in her approach and generous with praise.
O   She is on going in her commitment to Alpha Kappa Alpha Sorority, Incorporated.
L   She loves God, her family, her sisters and her neighbors as herself.
D   A golden soror is daring and dauntless.
E   She is earnest, enduring and endearing.
N   A golden soror is a nurturer of new sorors, all sorors and children.

S   She is sincere, sympathetic, dedicated to serve all mankind.
O   A golden soror is outgoing. She loves people.
R   A golden soror is a resource and she is resourceful.
O   She is on time on target and on top of all activities.
R   She is religious, reverent, and respectful of others.
S   She stands steadfast in "Holding High the Torch" and passing the light to others.

TO SOROR SARAH G. BRITTON
CONGRATULATIONS ON BECOMING A GOLDEN SOROR
March 31, 2007

S	Sincere and Sisterly
A	Active and Articulate
R	Regular in Attendance
A	Admired by all Who Know Her
H	Helpful and Hopeful
G	Golden Soror Of 2007
B	Believer in the concepts of AKA
R	Responsive to all chapter activities
I	Inspires Others
T	Trustworthy
T	Truthful
O	Optimistic
N	Natural Leader

PRESENTING THE FIRST SILVER STARS OF LAMBDA PHI OMEGA CHAPTER
March 31, 2007

You have been faithful members
Through thin and thin,
You have served your chapter
Your sorors can say "Amen."

You have captured a vision fair
Spreading service to all mankind.
Performing your purpose without any fears
Throughout your twenty five years.

You are Active sorors,
You are Kind sorors
You are Ambitious sorors
Sorors of AKA.

Now it's time to wear your Silver Crown
With a feeling of love and pride.
We respect and rejoice in your renown,
Lambda Phi Omega Sorors are on your side.

SILVER STARS 2006
Soror Gloria Berry
Soror Joyce Chappelle
Soror Reba Denmark
Soror Maryalyce Florence
Soror Helen Humphrey
Soror Doris Olukoya
Soror Bobbie Reeves
Soror June Sutton
Soror Ramona Davis

Now look ahead to twenty five more years of serving AKA.

SOROR CYNTHIA GOODRUM, EPISTOLEUS

Shaker Heights Library: Reader of the Month Cheryl Darden
Occupation: Educator/Supervisor in Special Education Department of the Cleveland Municipal School District
Lives in: Lomond neighborhood
Uses: Main Library and Bertram Woods Library
All time Favorite Book: In Search of our Mothers' Garden by Alice Walker
Likes to read: Fiction, mystery, magazines, autobiographies
Doesn't like to Read: Science Fiction
What I like best about the Library: The many activities the library sponsors. There is something offered for every age group throughout the year.
Other interests: Bowling, sewing, listening to music, billiards, shopping.
Family: husband, Theodore, retired lab technician, son Theodore, 19 (SHHS '05) a student at Youngstown State University and Cuyahoga Community College.
Volunteer Work: Moreland on the Move Community Association, Alpha Kappa Alpha Sorority, Incorporated. For the past nine years, Darden has organized the panel of judges for the Library's Dr. Martin Luther King Jr. Student Writing Contest and has read more than 3000 essays.
Brief Bio: Darden grew up in Cleveland and graduated from Shaker Heights High School (Class of '72). She received a B.S. ED from Ohio State University; M.ED from Cleveland State University and has been employed with the Cleveland Municipal School District for the past 31 years.

AKA IVIES BEYOND THE WALL

IVY BEYOND THE WALL
1980

The Ivy is strong, serene and pure,
The Ivy is green, enduring and true.
It is symbolic of the bonds of sisterly love,
Like unconditional, lasting, love from above.

The Ivy Vine climbs higher every day,
It does not grow in an ordinary way.
Its vines entwine, its leaves unfold.
As it strives to reach its goal.

It looks ever toward the bright sun,
That is the way the plant's work is begun.
Pushing ever upward, sturdy and strong,
Reaching for the heights where it belongs.

Soror Juanita E. Johnson, your life was like the Ivy Vine,
Faithfully striving to serve all mankind.
You always saw the bright side of things,
We know you are wearing your heavenly wings.

Lambda Phi Omega will never be the same,
You are with the Lord on a higher plane.
We will meet again on that distant shore,
Where partings and sorrows will be no more.

MY FRIEND AND SOROR SUSIE L. RICE

In 1978, Susie and I became traveling buddies. We attended AKA Clusters, Regionals and Boule' Conferences.

We would leave from Cleveland with a full tank of gas and hit the highway. Did you know that Susie liked to speed? Well she did, but she was a good driver. The truck drivers kept us informed as to where the traffic police were. They would say "Slow down Sweet Sue the man is ahead." We kept the communication open until we reached our destination.

Getting gas on the way or filling up when returning home presented a problem. Neither of us learned to fill our tanks when the stations put in self serve. Fortunately, some gentleman always came to our rescue when they would see us struggling with the operation.

Susie as a good Samaritan and helped all of her friends through serious illnesses'. She would visit them daily, rain or shine, sick or well. She helped them close their homes and locate to a nursing facility. She stayed and helped to the end. In 2002, when I fell in the garage and broke my right arm and my left knee, she stubbornly insisted that Bob bring her to visit. I didn't want her to because I knew how ill she was at this time. We were talking every day by phone. But this was Susie!

Susie and Bob loved animals. They always had pets, a dog and a cat. Susie always fed the birds.

Bob and Susie were hosts on a grand scale. They were both excellent cooks and referred to each other as Mama and Papa. Whether it was a formal dinner or backyard picnic we had unforgettable times together.

Susie was a horticulturist. There were flowers blooming inside and out. The roof would have hanging baskets of blooming gardenias and other blooming flowers. Bob was the gardener and planted vegetables of all kinds and generously gave them to friends. Susie loved to receive flowers from friend's, sorors and the chapter. During her illness, she stubbornly refused to throw out withered ones from Lambda Phi Omega. There was one she kept by her bed.

Susie took pride in decorating the display table for Pearl Day, MIP, and Founder's Day with her favorite candelabra. She was very proud of the AKA lighted emblem which Bob made and is still in use at all of our private and public functions.

Susie was also a politician. She was a member of Woodmere Council. She was Chairman of AKA Connection for her Chapter and she worked in high schools to register students to vote.

She was also the second Basileus of Lambda Phi Omega Chapter.

S   Susie a soror sincere and strong.
     Who lifted her voice in Praise and song.

U   She understood the AKA creed,
     Always to serve and help those in need.

S   She was sensitive to the principles of AKA.
     Always striving to keep the theme that way.

I   She was an inspiration to young and old.
     Innovative Inventive and always bold.

E   She stimulated energy in others,
     Had high expectations as a mother.

R	In appearance, she was stunningly royal, Her friendship was true and loyal.
I	She was intuitive and ready to help, Intentionally going an extra step.
C	Caring for others was her concern, All who knew her, could this discern.
E	Susie entered the ethereal gates, Finding joy eternal where Bob awaits.

A TRIBUTE TO SOROR JUANITA E. JOHNSON
Mount Zion Congregational UCC
March 30, 2005

Juanita E. Johnson has fought a good fight,
She has earned the right to say to us,
Her husband, her family, friends and sorors:

I have finished my race,
I have met my Saviour face to face.

Remember the years we spent together,
Mostly good but sometimes bad weather.

To my husband, Wright, I want to say,
Honey, I loved you every day and every way.

Don't grieve for me too long,
I want you to be happy and strong.

I want you and the family to draw closer
To God, love and respect each other's law.

Jesus said "Let not your heart be troubled;
Believe in God. Believe also in me."

I go to prepare a place for you I will come
again and will take you to myself. And where
I am you may be also.

So here I am, Wright with Ruth, our child,
Mother of Robert Jr. and Renee.
She greeted me with a welcoming smile.

A TRIBUTE TO SOROR DORIS J. GRANT
February 6, 2002

To the family: Lambda Phi Omega Chapter extends deepest sympathy for the loss of your loved one.

To all the people in the chapel: We share your feelings of grief and loss. At the same time you are a testimony by your presence of the love and regard we share for Doris J. Grant as we celebrate her "Home Going."

Jesus said, "In my Father's house there are many mansions, if it were not so, I would have told you. I go to prepare a place for you, and if I go and prepare a place for you I will come again and receive you unto myself; that where I am, there you will be also." Doris has entered the mansion prepared for her. She has fought the good fight; she has won the race.

The letters in her name will describe our tribute, love and regard for her.

- **D**   Dedicated, diligent, a Disciple of God, Devoted mother, grandmother, soror and friend.
- **O**   Outstanding leader and member of numerous organizations.
- **R**   Reliable, religious, reverent, respectful and resourceful.
- **I**   Inspiration to all who knew her.
- **S**   Sincere, sympathetic, sisterly and successful in all her endeavors.

- **J**   Joyful and a joy to be with.

- **G**   Generous with time, talent and treasure in giving service to all mankind.
- **R**   Respected the rights of others, always.
- **A**   Amiable, kind and articulate.

N   Never said "no" to a need.
T   Trustworthy and wanted on every team.

    A copy of this tribute is given to the family and a copy for Lambda Phi Omega's Archives.

TRIBUTE: TO SOROR RUTH COLLINS IVY BEYOND THE WALL
February 29, 2003

To Rose and the family of our beloved soror Ruth Collins, Lambda Phi Omega Chapter extends deep heartfelt sympathy. We feel your pain and grief because we have lost a beloved sister too. May God comfort and help you through this difficult time. Ruth's sorors are here to help you in any way we can.

Ruth was initiated into Alpha Kappa Alpha Sorority, Incorporated at Ohio State University. There she met Soror Susie Rice who would be here if she were able to give this tribute to Ruth.

After graduation, Ruth returned to Cleveland and Susie moved to Cleveland. Their friendship flourished and both became members of Alpha Omega chapter.

Much later Ruth became of member of Lambda Phi Omega Chapter where Susie was a Charter Member.

She was a dedicated soror and took part in all activities until her illness. She willing shared her outstanding musical talents and her time. Her superb soprano voice thrilled so many people. She also touched the lives of children, directing The Lafayette Elementary School Primary Choir for 27 years.

She was active in several community theater performances. She had a leading role in Langston Hughes' play, "Simply Heavenly," a musical comedy that had three runs at Karamu Play House.

She directed the" Pearl" a choral group of Lambda Phi Omega Chapter for 24 years.

In 1994, when the Cleveland chapters hosted The Great Lakes Regional Conference, Ruth wrote the lyrics for the song of Invitation. It was a smashing hit.

Soror Ruth was a Golden Soror giving over 50 years of active service to Alpha Kappa Alpha Sorority, Incorporated.

TO MY SOROR AND FRIEND
June 12, 1987

R   Ruth is remembered and recognized tonight,
As a reliable, resourceful teacher with foresight.

U   She has utilized her unlimited skill,
With an unselfish, uncompromising will.

T   Titillating, tantalizing, terrifically talented, she shines,
Touching tender, all these traits so wonderfully combined.

H   She is helpful, hopeful, honest and strong,
She heals your hurt when things go wrong.

C   Creative, caring, a courageous, compassionate COLLINS girl,
Conducting choirs which puts an audience in a whirl.

O   She is out spoken for sure, out reaching, true!
Her humor is outrageous, through it all she's secure.

L   A loving daughter and sister, her family will attest,
Her love is lasting, the very best.

L   She is loyal to friends and all she holds dear,
Loyal to commitments, year after year.

I   Indefatigable, at work or play,
Imaginative, inspiring in every way.

N   No words can adequately relay
The nobleness which her deeds portray.

S   Sister Rose's sensitive playing to her superb soprano voice,
We give salutations with sincere hearts and rejoice.

THE FAMILY MEMBERS OF AKA

FORTY YEARS OF WEDDED BLISS
BILL AND GEN MAIDEN

G	Gloriously in love and a generous wife,
E	Everyone's confidante' in times of strife.
N	Naturally optimistic, and energetic always,
E	Elegant, eloquent, many roles she plays,
V	Vibrant and vivacious, a gem of a mate,
A	An Anniversary of forty years to date.
A	And there were three children,
N	Nurtured by this union,
D	David, Little Gen. and Hasani.
W	Wonderful husband and a wise father,
I	Industrious, a self motivated starter.
L	Loving parent and a loyal companion to Gen.
L	Lasting and likable friend.
I	Interesting, and a very good singer,
A	Arduous in work or play,
M	Maker of good wine, too, some would say.
M	A milestone of FORTY WEDDED YEARS,
A	An achievement that calls for cheers.
I	In forty years, there were good times and bad,
D	Devoted and determined, they overcame the sad.
E	Enthralled and enchanted you more than ever portray,
N	Noble traits that produce such a day.

Happy Fortieth Wedding Anniversary!

DEDICATED WITH LOVE AND CONGRATULATIONS ON YOUR FIFIETH WEDDING ANNIVERSARY- PARENTS OF SOROR REBA DENMARK
October 22, 1982

B	Blist and blissful was Birdie's wedding day,
I	Inspired and imbued with love in a special way.
R	Respected and revered by all her peers,
D	Delightful, dutiful wife and a mother most dear.
I	Instructing her children with her imaginative mind,
E	Entrusting, enduring but always sweet and kind.
A	An admirable, adorable team,
N	Nurturing their children,
D	Devoted to a dream.
R	Rocelious was filled with rapture supreme,
O	On winning the sweetheart of his dream.
C	Children were born to this blessed pair,
E	Each was wanted and given loving care.
L	Life was filled with ups and downs, for a while,
I	In conquering problems, you responded with a smile.
O	Onward and onward, the years went by,
U	United by your faith in all kinds of weather,
S	Serene in your love, secure in being together.
G	Greetings we bring you at this time,
O	On your fiftieth Wedding Day Sublime.
O	Outstanding example, are you, of what marriage can be,
D	Doses of drama, spiced with many daring deeds,
S	Satisfaction gained from sharing your needs.
O	Of the years ahead, we wish you the best.
N	Nothing but happiness in your cozy nest.

SUSIE'S LETTER TO BOB
Wyllene B. Wall

Jesus said, "In my Father's House are many mansions. I go there to prepare a place for you for where I am, you shall be also." John 14: 1-3. Bob, I know you are there in that place. I felt you slip away Sunday evening February 8, 2004 around five o'clock. I was sleepy and didn't feel well but I realized a drastic change had taken place in my life. My doctor, caretakers and friends thought it blest to wait for Brenda Sue to arrive to break the news to me that you had gone to heaven. Only you and God can understand that a light has gone from my life.

I thank the Lord for all the precious and happy years we spent together. You were a true follower of Jesus Christ, not only in words but in deeds; the perfect husband and AKA Honey Do; a model father; a loving brother and uncle; A dedicated Alpha Phi Alpha brother and a faithful friend.

Bob, do you realize that we spent most of our lives together!!! I always thought I would be the first to go since I've been ill longer. But God knows what he is doing. He knows what is best for all of his children.

After eleven years we were blessed with Brenda Sue. She was five when we moved to Woodmere in 1961. Brenda celebrated her 6th Birthday party and received her first puppy, a little mutt that she dearly loved.

Bob, my mind goes back to when we lived with your mother on South Boulevard. I can see you there with your mother and also my mother and other relatives who have passed on. I'm sure they are there too.

Bob, you know I'm not very strong,
So the time will not be long,

*'Til I shall see you face to face,
Oh, the peace and joy in that happy place.*

Your Loving Wife, Susie

TRIBUTE TO OBAY OLUKOYA
JULY 22, 2008

O   Obay has crossed over,
         He is now at peace.

B   He was a brave brilliant person,
         Whom Doris loved very much.

A   He was attentive and he admired
         Doris' aspirations in so many areas.

Y   Yes, he was a good husband.

O   He was outstanding in the way
         He cooperated with her.

L   He loved the life they shared.

U   Bayo, was understanding and upright.

K   They shared a kind, kindred spirit.

O   Bayo, had an outgoing personality,
         Outstanding as a husband.

Y   Yes, you are going to miss him,
         But you will meet again never to depart.

Soror Doris, keep active, attend to your aspirations and remain alert to God's agenda for you. Remember all your sorors are here for you.

A FEW SHORT STORIES

DUST OFF YOUR DREAMS - IT'S NEVER TOO LATE

Fortunate are those persons whose first priority was/is accomplishing their dream. Not like others, and I include myself who have let every thing prevent them from pursuing the dream. First let me finish my education, get a job, marry, raise a family. Yet these people suffer nagging thoughts or moods that something is missing. You have your dream. I have my dream. I believe each of us has a dream. "All our dreams can come true if we have the courage to pursue them." said Walt Disney. Napoleon Hill said, "Whatever, the mind of man can conceive and believe, it can be achieved." If you have a dream that still exists, muster the courage to go after it.

Consider what the world would be like without the dream of Alexander Bell Graham who in 1874 at the age of 18 envisioned the idea of transmitting speech by electric waves. March 10, 1876 he became the inventor of the telephone with the words ' Watson, come here, I want you.'

The Wright brothers, Wilbur and Orville made the first powered flights in history at Kitty Hawk.

Recently, I was amazed and inspired about the story of a single parent coming to this country with a 7th grade education and two young boys. She worked hard at menial jobs and managed to raise and educate her boys. They earned scholarships to college, which was a big financial help.

When the boys graduated from college. She said, "Now I can finish school." One son said, "Mother why not try for the GED?" She did and passed. She enrolled in college and received a BS degree. Naturally, her economic status changed and she continued her studies earning a MA degree. When the article appeared in the news she had just received her Ph. D at the age of 89. She had patience, stamina, courage and persistence to realize her dream.

Never put off until tomorrow what you can do today," was a favorite epigram of my Grandmother, Patsy, "Procrastination is the thief of time," was another of her favorite wise Sayings. Marge is a typical example. The bright sun is shining trough the hazy in need of cleaning. Marge says to herself, "I will tackle the jobs tomorrow." This applies to dusting, baking cookies and changing beds that she can't do of course until she does the laundry.

"I can't miss another painting class." she reminds herself. "I should organize daily chores so that I have time for painting and class," she decides.

This decision was the start of her success as an illustrator of books for children and for greeting cards.

Anna Mary Robertson, a farmer's wife and widely known as Grandma Moses did not start painting until her late seventies. Grandma Moses had many exhibits throughout the United States and Europe. She died in 1961 at the age of 101. Her autobiography, "My Life History," was published in 1952. This late bloomer's work is noted for harmonious arrangement of figures and simple decorative treatment.

You might be thinking, these are people who had / have talent and you are right they are. I believe that each of us is given gifts by our creator. My belief is based on the parable in Matthew 25:14-30. The parable relates to money (the largest issue of currency in use at that time.) However, as word usage evolved, we have come to relate the word money to abilities. The master in the parable expected his servants to exercise their abilities as they used the five talents, the two talents, or the one talent he gave them. Scripture states, the master gave to each one according to his ability. As the story unfolds, the servant with the 5 talents doubled his to ten, the one with 2 doubled his to 4, but the one with 1 talent hid his in a safe place. He played it safe and consequently had nothing but the one talent that had been given to him. This parable is telling us whoever we are, whatever our talents great or small we should use them. That dream is your talent. If you have hidden it, now is the time to find it and bring it out.

Another inspirational character is Marian Anderson, who not only had to cope with her personal fears but she had to face the stigma of race discrimination. She was educated at the Chicago College of Music and in Europe. In 1925, she won first prize in a competition for an appearance with the New York Philharmonic Orchestra. Her reputation was established through a concert tour of Europe in 1933. After that she toured the United States and Europe extensively and sang with many leading symphony orchestras. In January 1955, she made her debut at the Metropolitan Opera House, New York City, in the role of Ulrica in "The Masked Ball," by the Italian composer Giuseppe Verdi. This was the first appearance of an African American singer with the Metropolitan Opera Company. Her autobiography, "My Lord What a Morning" was published in 1956.

Make a decision and don't waiver. Dust off your dreams - Its Not Too Late. The following eight steps might make your change a little easier. Focus on the dream every day. Formulate plans to make the dream happen. Then work your plan. Visualize the dream as a reality. Be optimistic. Believe in yourself. Pray for success.

I can't recommend a better time than now to start. Don't procrastinate another day. Remember procrastination is the thief of time. The dream is still alive and so are you. Remember, also that your dream fulfilled will make You and this world a better place.

WILMA'S PAIN

The night before August 12, 1999 Wilma Kelley had gone to bed perfectly well and slept through the night without any problem. She awoke at 7:30 the next morning, unable to get up. Alarmed and frightened she called for her husband, James who was in the bathroom.

"James," she screamed, "I think Mr. Arthur has me in his clutches, I can't move!" James helped his wife take a shower thinking it would help. After rubbing her down with Maximum strength Flexall, Wilma felt no better. She noted that the pain was not in her joints. It was more like a weakness in her pelvic muscles and upper arms. Needless to say, she did not take her usual walk that day or the next.

Sitting, standing, and walking were impossible. After two miserable days, the next step was to Dr. Gregory Hall, who gave her a physical including blood work. Two days later she was back in the office for the results. Her enzyme sediment rate (ESR) was 104 and the diagnosis, Polymyalgia Rheumatica (PR). Dr. Hall prescribed Predison 20 Mg. He asked her to take one pill as soon as she had the prescription filled and to call him an hour after taking the medication to let him know how she felt. Wilma did this and in an hour all the pain had completely disappeared. Dr. Hall then assured her that she did indeed have Polymyalgia Rheumatica and would need treatment for about two years.

If you are fifty years of age or over, female and Caucasian you need to read about this little known disease that can strike suddenly at any time.

"Sometime the disease goes away as mysteriously as it came. Again it might go into remission only to return," Dr. Hall explained. Wilma who had never heard of it was determined to find out all she could about it. "Dr. Hall have you treated any patients recently with PR?" Wilma asked. "No," he replied. "Last week, I had a similar presentation, but the lab did not confirm the diagnosis, in my eight years of practice you are the second person I've diagnosed." Wilma asked, "Do you know if more African American women than white suffer with this disorder?" "It's about equal," he replied. Wilma was persistent with her questions. "How can we make the public aware of the symptoms?" "Some people might think its arthritis or aches and pains that are associated with growing older and don't seek medical help." "I only realized after two days that it could not be arthritis because the pain was not in my joints," she reminded him. "Yes," Dr. Hall continued, "the symptoms are pretty vague, but quite severe. The most common being a unilateral headache (Giant Cell Arteritis). Clinical features of Polymyalgia Rheumatica include pain (usually bilateral and symmetric) in shoulder and pelvic girdle which is associated with stiffness, especially in the morning or after inactivity. As in patients with Giant Cell Arteritis, the ESR is usually elevated but up to 20% of patients may have normal or minimally elevated levels. Treatment with low dose glucocorticoids leads to prompt relief of Myalgias. It occurs in older people and women more than men. It is very important to see your doctor. Giant Cell Arteritis can lead to blindness if untreated. It is one of the select few disorders that if treated, give a dramatic improvement quickly. Other than treating infection with antibiotics, few other treatments have such a visible and quick response. That is why I asked you to call me an hour after your first dose of Prednisone," he concluded.

The interview ended with Dr. Hall saying he was sorry that there was not more information. He thanked Wilma for wanting to help others with the disease.

After six months of treatment Wilma became concerned about the side effects of Prednisone. Her blood pressure became elevated, her glucose level went up and there was swelling in her feet and ankles and a noticeable weight gain. She was especially anxious about diabetes because her grandmother had died from the disease.

Dr. Hall gave her medication to treat the hypertension and swelling. For the threat of diabetes and weight he suggested that she eat as if she were a diabetic. Over a period of time this worked, her glucose returned to normal and she lost weight. Dr. Hall decreased the dosage of Predisone until Wilma was taking only ten milligrams.

About this time, Dr. Hall referred Wilma to Dr. David Mandel, a noted Rheumatologist who gave her a battery of tests and concluded that Dr. Hall's diagnosis was correct and his treatment was proper. Wilma asked, "Dr. Mandel how many patients have you treated with this disorder?" He replied, "I am beginning my twentieth year of practice and I have treated approximately five hundred patients only twenty African American women. It is not as common in African American women. However, the genetics are still being researched."

"One encouraging fact," he continued, "Polymyalgia Rheumatica is not a life threatening disorder it is a disabling one if not treated. You are receiving the best that medicine has to offer at this time. About 95% of people respond to treatment starting with 15 milligram of Predisone per day and gradually tapering off after many months."

Dr. Mandel suggested that more information could be provided by the Arthritis Foundation of North East Ohio Chapter, located at 23811 Chagrin Blvd., Cleveland, Ohio 44122. Another source for information is the Internet, Rheumotology.Org.

Anyone experiencing any pain especially a sudden attack, should seek medical help immediately.

At the time of Wilma's incident with Polymyalgia Rheumatica, she was 62 years of age, healthy, having never suffered anything worse than a cold. She did not take medication, her blood pressure was normal. She was very active walking an hour daily and enjoyed a weekly exercise and line dance class.

Dr. Hall continued to monitor Wilma and gradually decreased Prednisone to ten mg. which was comfortable for her. She resumed her usual activities feeling great and very thankful.

Finally the day came when Dr. Hall decided to wean Wilma off the Predisone. He first started her taking one pill every day for a week and increasing the number of days between medication until she was taking it once every seven days. "Now," Dr. Hall announced, "Let's see what happens, stop the dosage!" Wilma did and today, she is free from pain and her ESR level is normal. She has been free from pain for three months and even if the disorder strikes again she knows what to expect and what to do.

Wilma desire is to raise the public's awareness about the pain. She hopes her story will accomplish this.

A LIFE TRANSFORMED

Where You Send Me I Will Go

Cold and aching, Vincent Harris awoke and stared out from beneath his card box suite snuggled up against a bridge column on New York City's 73rd Street. The frosty January air had brought shivers throughout the night and memories of pneumonia that had almost taken his life were running through his mind.

Suddenly he became aware that his body was demanding more drugs. He thought about his mother stating that she was "absolutely through "with him. " I'm not giving you another penny to help you kill yourself!"

'That's precisely what I'll do—kill myself,' thought Vincent. 'I'll take all my pills with a bottle of whiskey.'

He pulled himself together and walked down to Blessed Sacrament Church. The priest had allowed him to sit in the pews during the day for the two years he had been living on the streets. Slumped in the church pew, Vincent began to ponder how and why he had arrived at this point in his life.

Vincent was born in Manhattan on the Lower East Side and reared in a strict but loving home. His mother provided the best education sending him to St. Gregory Catholic Church for eight years. He reflected on witnessing many fights and slayings from his bedroom window. He recalled countless times when the priest would enter the classroom, and beckon him to serve at a funeral, usually, that of a gang member stabbed or thrown off a building. His heart began to pound as he remembered all the horrible things he had seen during the first fourteen years of his life.

Vincent's mind flashed back to his high school days at Rice High School. He recalled the strictness and how much he hated it. From a strict home with love to a strict high school without love held few happy memories for Vincent.

Vincent was a bright student and earned a scholarship to Herman H. Lehman College in the Bronx. He chose a job on Wall Street with Bankers Trust. "And that's where it all began," Vincent muttered to himself, " those lunches where everyone drank their lunch and shared joints. Marijuana had to be all right, if all the guys in their three piece suits were doing it.

Vincent hated his job dealing with stocks and bonds. He received a letter from Lehman that his scholarship would be forfeited if he didn't use it the following semester. It was a good time for him to go to college.

Vincent muttered, "I don't know how I managed to get a degree in 31/2 years doing drugs every day. I lost the opportunity to become an attorney. Stoned, I slept through the Law Scholarship Aptitude Test."

After graduation, Vincent went into a deep depression and began selling dope. Over the next two years he made plenty of money and lived in a luxury apartment on Central West. On the inside, he was empty and miserable. He recalled the time he prayed for God to help him do something constructive to make his family proud, especially his mother.

In 1979, working as a waiter on Amtrak, he was shown how to freebase cocaine. He quit Amtrak but he was addicted to cocaine.

One day he was freebasing in Harlem, a friend introduced him to heroin. "Speed balling" heroin on cocaine became routine. Now he was addicted to two drugs.

He thought about a prayer, he offered up about this time. 'Lord please give me the strength of slow this down so that I'm not spending more than $500 a day on drugs!" His habit had grown to $1,000 a day for cocaine and heroin. Vincent estimated he'd spent $250,000 for drugs in a period of 1 1/2 years.

Vincent supported his habit by shoplifting; living with pickpockets and just about anything else he could do to get his hands on cash.

He slept in Central Park, Port Authority or Grand Central Station most of the time. He rummaged trash bins for food to eat not wanting to waste cash on food.

"Yeah, anything to get some cash," Vincent muttered to himself on the pew, remembering the Christmas tree he had stolen and sold to get drugs after the hospital last month.

Vincent looked up from his temporary haven to see the priest motioning to him that it was time to leave. Slowly he made his way out of the stately doors and back to the bridge on 73rd Street.

As he approached his cardboard abode, Vincent fell to his knees praying. The words were coming from his mouth but it was as if he was listening to himself speak. "Almighty God in the name of Jesus Christ, I know this life I'm leading is not your will for me. I know you don't want me to commit suicide. Dear God there is no way I can break this addiction myself. Everything I've tried has failed. Lord, I am a sinner and I commit my life to you, to follow you to the four-corners of the earth if you want me to. Please break this addiction in my life.

Although, he didn't realize it until Later, Vincent slept that night without drugs. The following day he dashed to the rich white sector of Park and Fifth Avenues to sift through garbage cans for anything of value that he could sell. He raised $40. Vincent went to a local shelter to get deloused. Two street men told him of a homeless shelter in Greymoor, N.Y. operated by Catholic Priests who would help people.

Vincent made a beeline to the bus station and bought a ticket for $8.50 only to be informed that the next bus was the following day. He lay down on a Port Authority bench and went to sleep. Hours later he awoke to find someone had picked his pocket of all his cash. Furious Vincent stuck his hands further in his pocket. Amazingly the bus ticket was still here.

When he arrived at Greymoor, Father Charles listened carefully to Vincent's story. "You will have to stay here until there is an opening at Saranac Lake," he explained.

On the third morning at Greymoor, Vincent awoke with a strange feeling. He was on fire from his neck to his waist. The burning sensation was so intense, he could hold his hands twelve inches from his chest and feel the heat shoot off his body. In a panic, Vincent jumped up to locate a nurse. He heard a voice, say "stand still." Vincent obeyed. Instantly, serenity, calm, a sense of well-being, flooded through him. That moment, he knew the obsession to use drugs was completely gone.

Vincent followed through with 52 days at Greymoor, and then 90 days at St Joseph for group therapy and individual counseling. Next he went to a half way house in Syracuse. Vincent was hired to do specific cleaning duties to maintain the facility. Eventually, Vincent shared his story with Father O'Brian, who asked him to help out in a homeless shelter in Syracuse. From this step, he was asked to help in a state program called Vised. Because of Vincent's testimony, background and attitude, Vised paid for his schooling and special training at Syracuse University. Two and a half years later, Vincent became a certified substance abuse counselor of New York State. Shortly, he was hired as a Counselor at Syracuse Community Health Center. He was doing referrals for both the Catholic and Protestant churches in the area. A friend introduced him to Dr. Hazel Roper, an area representative and associate minister of the American Baptist Churches. Dr. Roper recognized special gifts in Vincent and began taking him to several area churches. "I was practically living in church," laughs Vincent. "Every day I went straight from work to church or a revival. I was so thirsty for God's Word that I couldn't seem to get enough."

At Hobbs Memorial Baptist Church in Syracuse, he became a friend with the pastor, Larry Howard. "God is calling you to the ministry, Vincent, but you need more education," Rev. Howard advised. After considerable encouragement, Vincent wrote to Colgate Rochester Divinity School and received an invitation to a ministry conference. He was accepted into the program with a grant of $6,400. In his second year, he served 11 months in Hong Kong, teaching substance abuse rehabilitation from a Christian perspective. Vincent realized his life was completely changed. "God has transformed me and I am prepared to go where ever He sends me," Vincent said humbly.

He returned home in 1995. Three years after entering Colgate, the former New York, homeless, heroin addict, graduated with a master's degree in divinity.

After serving as an interim pastor at Fabius Baptist Church, Vincent accepted the Chaplaincy at Thistledown Racetrack in Cleveland, Ohio in 1996." I simply feel at home on the track," said Vincent. "I know I'm right in the middle of God's perfect will."

THE VISION

My mother dropped the receiver, screamed and burst into tears. I ran to her starting to cry too. Between sobs she told me Aunt Cora who had been ill had just died and she hadn't gone home to see her. We would have to go home for the funeral. "Mama, we are home," I said. "No, baby, she replied, home is in Alabama where I was born and where most of our relatives live. I haven't been home since you were born almost six years ago. During this conversation, Mama was busy, pulling out suitcases and packing. She made several calls and finally explained we would be leaving the next day and would arrive at home the following day in time for the funeral.

The next evening, we boarded a fast moving passenger train for home. I was so excited and while it was still light, I kept my eyes glued to the window watching the changing scenery go by. The snow covered ground soon changed to brown. My first train ride, my first time going home. When I glanced at Mama, looking so sad I took her hand and held it. Why did Aunt Cora have to die and make my Mama cry?

Grandpa Nero's green rambling farmhouse with white shutters was crowed with people when we arrived, everyone talking at the same time. My mother's father, three sisters, Mary, Alma and Ethel and her only brother Ross greeted us with hugs, tears and kisses. Everyone was dressed and ready to go. Mama hurriedly changed into a black dress Aunt Ethel combed my hair and quickly dressed me in a blue jumper with a white blouse.

The members of Abraham Baptist Church stood as the family entered. The pastor quoted consoling scripture as we were seated in the front pew. Our family took up more than half the right side of the church. There was much crying, singing, praying and remarks by organizations and friends.

On the long ride to Snowden where Aunt Cora would be buried everyone was quiet and subdued lost in his or her own thoughts until after the casket was interned. As we left the cemetery, the mood lifted and the ride back didn't seem as long.

The crowd thinned out after we had eaten, leaving just the immediate family. Mama was tired and we soon went to bed. The twin bedroom was off to the right of the dining room where Mama and I slept. I lay awake long after Mama had closed the door and kissed me good night. As I lay there, the door opened and a figure dressed in flowing white appeared it seem to float or drift to the bed where Mama was sleeping. There it stood still for a while leaning over looking at Mama and then it floated to my bed and tucked the covers around me and drifted through the door leaving it open. I remember thinking before falling asleep that I must tell Mama about the visitor.

Mama hugged and kissed me when I told her about the visitor and said that it was a dream. The rest of the family looking strange agreed with Mama. But I realized when I was older, that Aunt Cora came to visit us that night.

CHURCH

I BELIEVE
February 18, 1999

1. In God's power, his love and his mercy.
2. In the compassionate nature of humanity.
3. That goodness overcomes evil.
4. In prayer, faith, hope as guides to daily living.
5. In peace and justice.
6. God appointed man to be stewards of his creation and his abundance.
7. In the second coming of Jesus Christ.
8. We should love everyone.
9. In giving of time talent and treasure to further god's kingdom.
10. In letting our light shine as a witness.
11. In helping those in need.
12. In the power of intercessory prayer.
13. In reading and listening to god's word.
14. We are responsible to see that all children are nurtured in love, faith and preparation for life.

Gifts from God
August 7, 1998

When you dwell among the stars,
No matter, who or where you are,
When you view the beauty of the earth
And each season witness its rebirth,
You have received a gift from God.

When you look in the face of an innocent child
Watch them play and see their smiles,
The gift of children is a treasure from God,
Help them to grow in love and faith from the start
Teach them, care for them, love them. Do your part.

BECOME A GUIDING LIGHT

G	Seek God's will for you
U	United Methodist – Uplifting missions
I	Listen to Inspiring Sermons
D	Become Dedicated Volunteers
I	Pray In earnest
N	Neighbors helping neighbors
G	Appreciate God's Generosity and Forgiveness
L	Love one another
I	Search for Images of Jesus Christ
G	Be thankful for God's Grace
H	Live with Hope and Humility
T	Teach children and Touch somebody's life
S	Attend Sunday School.

ESSENTIALS FOR PEACE WITH YOURSELF

1. Receive Christ as your personal Savior.
2. Believe and accept that God is absolute sovereign.
3. God is going to supply every single need you have.
4. Maintain a clear conscious.

EXCUSES FOR NOT GOING TO CHURCH
August 1975

I would go to church today,
But the service is too long,
The ball game very soon,
Church isn't out until afternoon.

I would go to church today,
But really it's so warm,
The beach is cool and shady,
I will go this winter, so what is the harm?

I would go to church today,
But outside it is very cold,
How cozy to stay snug inside
"Be comfortable," I've always been told,

And so it goes each Sunday
Excuse after excuse you give,
One by one each fades away,
Never again to be relived.

I would if I could go to church today,
Now I am ill and have time to pray
"Hear me, Lord for now I am old
I no longer dread the heat or the cold."

I would if I could go to church today,
"Dear Father, forgive my wasted life,
Now, Lord I can only pray,
Help me to go to church today."

WHAT IS WRONG WITH THE FIRST PEW
January 1976

What is wrong with the first pew?
It is usually empty,
Or occupied by a few,
Someday, when I get the nerve
I will find out what is wrong,
With the front pew.

TEACHERS
September 1975

Teachers lead as Jesus led
The Disciples in his day,
To spread the word
And show the world the way

Teachers with strength,
Convictions strong;
Willing to work
With enthusiasm and charm.

Teachers of Children,
Teachers of youth,
An understanding heart,
A searcher of truth.

WINDOWS
February 19, 1996

Windows look in and also out,
Either way, we see our world.
Looking without, we see

Homeless, hopeless people.
Desperate in their need.
Hungry, abused children.
Drug infested neighborhoods;
Poverty, violence and crime.

All this evil, we witness and discern,
It becomes our Christian concern.

We see the beauty of God's wonderful Creation
Slowly being destroyed.

Polluted air and water, killing life,
Natural resources, expendable and wasted,
Diseases raging and rampant in the world,
The ozone layer becoming larger, a potential danger,
Wars are still being fought, no peace in sight.

With all our wealth, science and technology,
We are unable, helpless, to save ourselves.

Looking within, we feel that ray of hope,
God is still in control

We need to pray and seek his directions,
As we try to make the right corrections
To heal brokenness and make society whole.
We need to heed His commandments,
Trust in his promised love and mercy
For all mankind.

Jesus is waiting for the world to run from sin
To obedience and belief of everlasting life through Him.

METHODIST MEN IN ACTION
September 1975

United Methodist Men so few and yet so strong,
This is to give tribute in a song.
Some of you are new and some are old,
Others are quiet while some are bold.
Whatever your thing happens to be
St Paul needs every one of you, you see.

U	is unity in working together,
N	is nurturing a desire to grow better,
I	are ideals lofty and true,
T	is temperance and keeping pure,
E	is the essence of a Christian life,
D	is devotion, first to God and then wife,

M	is mercy, one for the other,
E	is earnest Christian brothers,
T	is trust, talent and tact,
H	is keeping harmony and humor a fact,
O	is obligation, assumed today,
D	is the discipline to know and obey,
I	is the interest in which all share,
S	is service willingly spent,
T	is time given showing you care.

M	Ministers, Ministries, men and mission,
E	Every one to sing and pray
N	Needing God's help every day.

THAT WE MAY BE ONE IN CHRIST
ST. PAUL 52ND ANNIVERSARY
SEPTEMBER 1975

We must have love for all,
God's creatures great and small;
That we may be one in love.

We must have abiding faith,
That stands steadfast in every way,
That we may be one in faith.

We must have understanding,
A unity of purpose free for all,
That we may be ones who stand tall.

Sharing and working to make things better,
The goal we have made together,
That we may be one in purpose.

We must have undying hope,
That with all problems we will cope,
That we may be ones to share.

As we work and as we pray,
Guide our efforts so we cannot stray,
That we may be ones who care.

We reach out here at St. Paul,
Listen and heed our Christian call,
That we may be one reaching out to all.

WHO AM I?
August 1975

Who am I,
Dear Lord, I ask,
What can I do,
What are my tasks?

Who am I,
Just one small part,
Where do I fit,
Where shall I start?

Who am I,
Dear Lord, I pray,
That I am yours,
Use me today!

MOTHER HOOD
MAY 7, 1976

M	is for mother who
O	Overcomes obstacles to good moral values, using
T	Thought, time and tact, they also
H	Help with homework and human relations through
E	Education, experience and expertise
R	Reevaluate, review, renew rules with
H	Honesty, humility and prayer
O	Overpower opposition with love, faith and
O	Outstanding optimism combined with
D	Diligence, determination and devotion

THOMAS MCDANIEL'S DAY
OCTOBER 10, 1975

T   Is the time he spends in church,
singing, praying and doing much.

H   His heart, kind and true,
swells with love that is pure.

O   Opened minded in his thoughts,
Understanding which he sought;

M   The Master whom he loves,
whose mercy comes from above

A   Able to take each wrong,
make it right and emerge strong.

S   Sincerity of purpose and deed,
helping others in need.

M   Making coffee so well,
every one drinks it and says "it is swell."

C   Custodian who cares,
never complains which is rare.

D   Duties done each day,
efficient in his own quiet way.

A   Arranging seating for meetings,
as you arrive he smiles his greetings.

N   Nothing but helpfulness is his plan,
to help St Paul in every way he can.

I   Inspiration his life inspires,
through Christ he receives what he desires.

E	Everyone who helps make "His Day,"
	outstanding and successful in every way.
L	Leadership on the Usher Board,
	willingly carries a heavy load.
D	For Daniel in the Lion's den,
	he too found God a faithful friend.
A	Again for answering so many requests,
	in such a kind way he can't help but be blest.
Y	Yielding to God's will
	comforted by him and by him fulfilled.

WOMEN ON THE MOVE WOMEN'S DAY
May 1976

W   World wide women on the move, willing, wise and wonderful, who

O   Oversee, overview outlined objectives, observe and overpower elections.

M   Mocking the memory of days now past.

E   Ever growing echelon of efficient women, whose efforts in events are essential

N   Nothing now can stem the tide of their untapped potential and pride.

O   On going, out reaching, step by step measuring growth and inner depth,

N   Noting the need to lessen crime, negotiating for safety is how they use their time.

T   Taking hold in a tangible way, to solve the problems we face today.

H   Heed the movement, as they plod, hear their cry "give your heart to God."

E   Every woman, on God's earth embodies the essence of this rebirth.

M   Moving on, with a Christian mind, making friends and always kind.

O   One by one they move in sight, they have an option on what is right, with

V   Virtue, victory, and vivacious charm, they have visions of a world free from harm.

E   Emerging, effectively to eliminate sin, an elated Christian and an elegant friend.

MY PRAYER
September 26, 1973

Almighty God, give us grace to approach Thee at this time with penitent and believing hearts. Cleanse our thoughts and create in us a new spirit as we approach the altar this morning. We come before thee with various needs knowing you have the power to make everything alright.

In your great compassion, O Lord, you can comfort the unhappy, heal the sick and lighten the burdens of the weary. Be with us this morning as we humbly bow our heads in prayer.

Dear Heavenly Father, we are grateful for the many blessings that Thou hast bestowed upon us. O Lord, my God, we know that it is thy loving kindness and tender mercy that enables us to be here today. We are ever thankful for the opportunity to sing and give praise to Thee. Let Thy merciful ears, O Lord be open to the prayers of thy humble servants that we may obtain petitions. Make us to ask such things as shall please you.

Heavenly Father, we ask your blessings for, Pastor Raymond Burgess and all the leaders of our congregation, Strengthen them and give them the wisdom and understanding to make the right decisions. Bless our entire church family and help us to grow stronger in Christian love and brotherhood toward eachother and toward all mankind.

Dear Lord, throw your strong arm of protection around those who are ill and cannot be here this morning. We ask a special comfort for those who are confined in hospitals and for their families. Give them, O Lord, the courage to face their problems unafraid and with faith, knowing that they need only to trust in Thee.

Dear Heavenly Father, help us to perform our tasks in a manner that is pleasing in Thy sight. Grant us, O Lord, we beseech Thee, the spirit to think and do always only things that are right. Pour down upon us the abundance of Thy mercy we pray this morning.

O God, The protector of all, be with those who are taking part in the service this morning. Sustain and inspire the speaker who occupies the pulpit today.

Have compassion, Dear Lord, upon all of those who are heavily burdened, the poor, the lonely, the fearful and those who face danger. Heal, protect and strengthen them according to their needs if it is Thy Holy will.

Be with all of us if it is thy will Lord, for we need Thee every hour, Most Gracious Lord. There are those who stand humbly before this altar who need Thee. Thou, who can see in each heart and who knows all about us, fill each need, ease each pain and solve each problem, if it is Thy Holy Will or help us to bear our crosses bravely. O Lord, my God, forgive what we have been, help us to mend what we are and in Thy Spirit, O Lord, direct what we shall be so that in the days to come our actions will be pleasing in Thy sight This is our prayer. Amen

MOTHER
May 7, 1997

Dedicated to those who wear white flowers on Mother's Day

How tenderly Mom wiped away my tears,
When Mom was near, I had no fears.

Mom's kind eyes and her sweet voice,
In what happy memories I still rejoice.

Mom taught me, first to pray,
And how to live in a Christian way.

Games we played and stories Mom read,
She kissed me goodnight and tucked me in bed.

My mother was gentle but very strong,
She would not tolerate any wrong.

Mom was strict but always just,
How could I ever betray her trust?

As the years go by my memories grow bright,
For I remember my mother with much delight.

First Lady of St. Paul U.M.C. Mrs. Johnettra Burgess
May 15, 1975

She is the perfect mate
To Rev. Burgess, she can relate,
Our first Lady.
She is also an ideal mother,
To Rayna and Mira, she is like no other,
Our First Lady.
She teaches a class in Sunday School,
Always calm, collected and cool,
Our First Lady.
The piano, each Sunday, she plays,
In all activities, we enjoy her helpful ways.
Our First Lady.
She is the power behind the man,
Quietly doing all she can.
Our First Lady.
Today, Mrs. Burgess, we want you to know,
How dear and special to us, you daily grow.

MESSAGE TO VISITORS

V   Visitors, I am glad you came,

I   The Aldersgate family echoes the same.

S   Inviting you to come again,
           Joining in Worship will be your gain.

I   Inspiring this Service will be,
           A solace to you and a solace to me.

T   Teaching us to always trust
           Things that are true and just.

O   Obeying the commandments of Christian living,
           Obedient to God with generous giving.

R   Reaching toward righteousness always,
           Reverence not just Sunday, but all of our days.

S   Singing songs of love and praise,
           Studying God's word and seeking his grace.

Welcome to Our Church
It's warm in every way,
We all welcome you very much
Come often and sing and pray.

ST PAUL UNITED METHODIST CHURCH
UNITED METHODIST WOMEN
APRIL 1978

U	Unity in goals, the
N	Needy we help
I	Interested in knowledge,
T	Teaching team work, we are
E	Earnestly and eagerly
D	Diligently doing our duties.

M	Mustering our
E	Efforts together,
T	Thoughtful, ever
H	Honest endeavor,
O	Outstanding, optimistic, we are
D	Delightful dreamers,
I	Inspiring others,
S	Sincerely searching,
T	Trusting, touching

W	Worshiping, working, we are
O	Out reaching in
M	Missions, member and ministries
E	Enthusiastically engaged in
N	Neighborly and national pursuits

WOMEN'S DAY ST. PAUL UNITED METHODIST CHURCH
WOMEN WITH VISION
1979

If all the lazy women would get up,
And all the sleeping women would wake up,
And all the discouraged women would look up,
And all the gossiping women would shut up,
And all the fighting women would make up;
And all the mean women sweeten up,
And all United Women would show up,
And all church women pray up,
And all leading women line up,
And all back sliding women pay up,
And all Christian women speak up,
And all choir women sing up,
And all scared women won't back up,
Then St. Paul will be filled with "Women with Vision."

OCCASION
WOMEN'S DAY, ST. PAUL UMC
MAY 12, 1973

It is a real pleasure to extend a warm welcome to our visitors who have come to join in our worship service on Women's Day. Let us take a look at the word WELCOME.

W	Womanhood we admire,
E	The elegance of a woman's attire,
L	Her loyalty to her Christian faith,
C	For church, we worship and congregate.
O	Obey the commandments of God,
M	Our minister who guides us in,
E	Efforts we make to help and trust each other.

We hope that you will find the service uplifting and inspirational and that you will return to visit with us often. If you are seeking a church home, you might take a look at St. Paul. We may have just the kind of warm, friendly Christian atmosphere you have been looking for. Please be seated and thank you for standing.

MOTHER

Mother stood on the mountain top and watched the sun rise on a beautiful day. She was happy. She looked down into the valley. It was lush and green. There was work to be done and she toiled long. In the valley, she saw the sun set at the end of a beautiful day. It was dark and quiet but mother was happy. She had completed her work.

Her image was there,
Before I was aware,

Even as I cried,
Hungered and slept.

She calmed my fears
Fed and soothed me,
When I was ill,
With loving patient skill.

She taught my
Faltering steps,
To grow stronger,
With a pleasing smile.

WOMEN WITH VISION
Program "Women's Day," St. Paul UMC
May 21, 1978

Women with vision have their dreams,
Making them come true, takes more than schemes.
Women with vision learn to speak,
They know when to be strong and when to be meek.

Women with vision are full of love,
Sweet and soft like a beautiful dove.
Women with vision are fully aware,
Always optimistic which is very rare.

Women with vision you see them every day
Esther English, Myrtle Chavers, Ella Gray
Women with vision you see taking part,
Shirley LeCompte, Bertha Prater, Elsa Hart.

Women with vision, active and strong,
Juanita Parham, Carol Childress, Elaine Long.
Women with vision do what is right,
Reba Denmark, Barbara Rogers, Beauty White.

Women who sing give untold pleasure,
Dorothy Solomon, Ethel Dickerson, Nellie Lacy.
Their talents are truly a treasure
Women with vision, who have stood the test,
Marie Finch, Sue Drawn, Katherine West.

Women with vision, we can't name them all,
The Harpes, theWiggins, the Halls
The women with vision at St. Paul.
Women with vision are filled with hope,

Rebecca Bryant and Myra Pope.

Women with vision become involved,
Roslyn Miller, Lavada Bivins, Lucy Johnson
They are the ones who get problems solved.
Women with vision believe in prayer,
Ruth Wallace
They take their troubles to God who cares.

VALENTINE DAY
February 9, 1996

Love is a clap of thunder,
A voice in the wilderness
Calling us home.

Love is a song, music
A voice in the wilderness
Calling us home.

Love is a prayer of light,
Love is mighty in God's sight.
_____ you are a beloved leader.

Love is a song, music, a note, rhythm and rhyme,
Voices lifted in praise by all our choirs,
Their singing we love, appreciates and admire
We love all of you!
You are our "Singing Valentines!"

Love is the children,
Nurtured by Aldersgate's Church School.
Children's Sermons,Choirs and congregation
They are our precious Valentines!
God loves them and so do we!

Love is Aldersgate's Officers and leaders,
Who work with willing hands in God's Vineyard.
They keep focused on our goals
To magnify God's Kingdom.
We love you Leading Valentines!

Love is the Congregation
Whose worship is sincere and warm,

Praying, singing and hearing the word, together,
No Valentines could be better,
We love God, Ourselves and each other!

HAPPY VALENTINE DAY!

MY PRAYER

Dear God, please guide me day by day,
Guide my footsteps on their way.
Less I stumble and fall.

Help me to live a good clean life,
Unselfish and brave, overcoming strife,
For I would be free.

Give me the courage to reach out,
And speak with those I meet,
For I would love.

Give me the wisdom to think,
And the bravery to speak my thoughts,
For I would teach.

Give me joy and pride.
In your words I feel inside, for they come from you,
For I would write, if it be your will. Amen

LAITY PRAYER
October 11, 2005

O Lord as we daily walk with you,
As we daily talk with you.
Lord guide our footsteps on the way,
To serve and praise you every day.

Heavenly Father we love you and each other,
Help us to be one in Spirit, Sisters and Brothers.
Helping the poor, the sick and weak,
The homeless, the hungry, the lonely the meek.

We will tell them of Jesus and his love.
That Salvation comes from above
Our church is a Beacon, lighting the
The Pathway to you Almighty God.

Father, keep us strong, but humble,
Forgive us when we sin and stumble,
In the church we will find our place
To use the bestowed gifts of your grace.

O Lord, we meditate day and night,
To do what is pleasing in your sight.
To spread the word wherever we are
Accepting the love of Jesus is the first start.

This prayer we pray in the name of Jesus amen!

PRAYER OF CELEBRATION
John L. Wall

O God, Lent is a time of preparation for the celebration
of the Risen Christ who died to save the world. Thank
you Gracious Lord for the gift of your love and for your
only begotten son who gave us the free gift of Salvation.
Jesus Christ, the Light of the World, our Savior and Redeemer,
Will forever praise your holy name. Amen

MY DAILY PRAYER
Wyllene B. Wall

Sometimes, my heart is filled with joy,
So great it's hard to contain.
Again, my heart is filled with pain,
So severe it's hard to sustain.
"Oh, how I love Jesus,"
This is my daily refrain.

THIRD SUNDAY LIGHTING
THE PURPLE CANDLE-SHEPHERD
December 12, 1999

PRAYER WITH WORSHIP PARTICIPANTS

Heavenly Father, We thank you for this day, for getting us up this morning and sending us on our way. Lord, we just want to thank you and praise Your Holy name. Thank you Lord, for this opportunity to be of service in your name. We ask your blessing and your strength as we do what we have been called to do this day. Bless the Acolytes, Cassandra Jessie and Gannell Gray. The Greeters: Mabel Green, Eloyce Mercer, and Roberta Williams and the ushers. Be with Elaine Smith as she works with the children. Continue to empower the Angelic Choraliers under the direction of Afi Odelia Scruggs. O God we thank you for Diann Darby who will have moments with our children and Nancy Stephens who will be our Liturgist today. Help all of us to accept the challenge as laity to carry on in the absence of Pastor Benita.

Lord, help me, your humble servant to be a confident Lay Leader as I bring your message today. Lord I have faith that you will see me through. Thank you Lord for these moments together. In the name of your son and our Lord and Savior, we pray. Amen.

THE FAMILY PRAYS

Let the shepherds lead the way to the altar as we prepare to offer prayers of thanksgiving, prayers of petition and prayers of intercession. To our Heavenly Father. Come to the Altar, kneel or stand and pray your prayer, knowing that God hears. Leave your burden here. (2 Minutes).

Lord, this morning, grant the petitions of your people, we pray in Jesus' name.

Once again, O God, we lift our eyes unto the hills from whence cometh our help. Our help comes from you 0 Lord. We give you thanks and praise for your abundant blessings, eternal goodness and everlasting love. Heavenly Father, you are the gracious, generous provider of our every need and we thank you, Lord. You are so good to us, your mercy is everlasting and your truth endureth through all generations. Thank you Lord. Heavenly Father, forgive us our sins and strengthen us where we are weak. Help us to be more like Jesus and to do things the "Jesus Way."

O God, we pray that you will comfort and give peace to those who are ill, grief stricken, lonely, afraid, at Aldersgate and in the world, the homeless, the hungry the poor, the friendless who need your comforting healing touch.

Father God we pray that you would guide the hearts and minds of the leaders of churches, governments and schools everywhere so that the world can become one of peace and love. A world where children are safe from harm danger and violence, we pray in Jesus' name.

Lord our vision is to become a beacon lighting the pathway to you. Father continue to bless us in every way. Through family and friends and your loving care each day. Amen.

BENEDICTION:
And Now May The Blessing Of God Almighty, Father, Son And Holy Spirit, Be Among You And Abide With You, Now And Evermore. Amen.

LAITY LITANY
October 16, 2005

LORD WE ARE THE LAITY
We love honor and glorify you.
We need your strength to see us thru.

LORD WE ARE THE LAITY
We praise your name and worship you.
We feel your everlasting love so true.

LORD WE ARE THE LAITY
We are obedient and faithful unto you.
Your truth is everlasting from generation to generation.

LORD WE ARE THE LAITY
Our gifts and service we give to you.
Your commandments we obey and do.

Lord we magnify and glorify your precious name.

We praise and lift up your name throughout the earth.

STEWARDSHIP SUNDAY
December 29, 2002

Introduction

God has given to each of us, in varying amounts, his gifts of time, talents and treasure. We are stewards or caretakers of these gifts and have a responsibility to use them to help build up the kingdom of God to build a better world and a better church.

Belvia: Did you know that most people live on an eight day week- not a seven day week?

Wyllene & Louise: What do you mean Belvia?

Belvia: Most people, not people at Aldersgate thank goodness, have Sunday, Monday, Tuesday, Wednesday, Thursday, Friday, Saturday and Someday.

Wyllene: It does seem as if some of the most important things in life are reserved for Someday. I always say Someday; I'm going to compile all my writings. Someday has not arrived yet.

Louise: Yes, Someday we will visit a sick friend. Someday, we will consider what gift of time talent and treasure we ought to make to God's work

Belvia: Someday we will volunteer to sing in the choir, be an usher or serve on a church committee.

Wyllene: Someday we will submit an article to the Beacon or teach a Sunday School Class.

Louise: Someday, we will increase our giving or begin tithing.

Belvia: The grand tragedy of life is that Someday is never part of any week Someday never comes

Wyllene: Because Someday never comes, many of the important things in our churches never get done.

Louise: The work of God must never be a Someday project. Now is the time to make your commitment to the work of Christ.

All: What gift of talent time and treasure will you make to see that Christ's work is done on Sunday, Monday, Tuesday, Wednesday, Thursday, Friday, and Saturday during all of 2003?

REFLECTIONS ON VACATIONS (A RAP)

We go on vacation every year.
We leave for places far and near,

Summer is peak vacation time!
Vacation from school.
Vacation from working,
Vacation from playing
Vacation from just about everything!

Why do we plan vacations?
We need a rest, A change of pace,
A change of scenery
Just a chance to get away from it all!

How do we travel?
We go by air,
We go by car,
We travel by ship,
We go by train,
Or we go by bus.

What do we do on vacation?
We flock to the beaches,
And picnic in the park,
We never stop going
From sun-up to dark,
We go sightseeing,
We also shop,
We swim and play
Until we almost drop.

Suppose God, Jesus and the Holy Ghost took a two week vacation! Could that happen? What would we do?
There would be no one to look after us, protect us, provide for us,
Our songs would be sung unheard by heaven,
Our prayers would go unanswered too,
Our strength, faith, and trust would also weaken,
Who would we turn to when all else failed?

But it's really wonderful that God, Jesus and the Holy Ghost never go on vacation! They never leave us alone!
Vacations are for folks like us,
But God is always home!

The church does not go on vacations either!
Although its members do
How will the Church survive when lights, gas
And other bills come due?
While you are enjoying your vacation
Remember your church needs you,
Remember your church depends on you!
YOU! YOU! YOU!

MY PRAYER

Dear God, please guide me day by day, Guide my footsteps on their way Less I stumble and fall.
Help me live a good clean life,
Unselfish and brave, overcoming strife, for I would be free.
Give me the courage to reach out, and speak with those I meet,
For I would love.
Give me wisdom to think,
And the boldness to speak my thoughts, for I would teach.
Give me joy and pride,
In your words, I feel inside,
For they come from you.
Help me to form the words,
For I would write,
If it is your will.

THE ME: FROM JERUSALEM TO THE WORLD

Let us tell the story,
Spread the "Good News."
Of God's love and redemption,
For all the world to hear.
Tell the story by word,
Lift it up in song,
Practice it in deeds,
Show it electronically,
Tell it any way you can,
Tell it all along life's pilgrim journey.
Spread the "Good News,"
Of Jesus, Lord and Savior,
So the whole world can know,
And be redeemed.

STEWARDSHIP SUNDAY
July 30, 2006

We Are The Church
You Are The Church
We Are The Church Together,
We Work To Make It Better.
We Love And Cherish Each Other:
The Babies In Our Midst,
The Children We Assist.
The Youth Who Are Receiving
The Young Adults Who Are Achieving
The Adults Who Stand Strong,
The Seniors Who Do No Wrong.
The Pastors Who Guide Us Along,
Thank You Almighty Lord!
We Are Aldersgate's Worshipers Together,
We Thank God For Surviving All Kinds Of Weather.
We Are The Church,
You Are The Church,
We Are The Church Together,
We Work To Make It Better
The Church Undergoes Wear And Tear,
We Are Stewarts Of This Repair.
All Of This Takes Revenue,
This Is What God Expects Us To Do.
To Have Lights There Is A Bill,
To Pay For This Is God's Will.
The Phones, The Church Can't Do Without,
We Must Communicate Without A Doubt.
An Efficient Secretary Does Not Come Cheap,
Her Skills And Expertise, Oh Lord, We Must Keep.
Our Custodian Works So Very Hard,
For Each Event He Plays A Part.

The Pastors, Music Directors, Choirs,
You Are The Nourishers Of Our Souls And Minds,
With Wise Teachings And Uplifting Songs Of All Kinds.
We are the church,
You are the church,
We are the church together,
We work to make it better.

Listen up church! Hear our Plea!

HARMONY AND BALANCE

When God completed the creation of the world, he looked around and said, "this is good." Everything was in perfect harmony. He had a right to be pleased. There were earth and sky. There were land and water, high hills and mountains, valleys and plains. There were deserts and green forests. The heavens changed smoothly into day, morning, noon evening and night. The sun shines during the day and the moon shines at night. The seasons change from spring to summer, fall and winter, All move in perfect harmony.

The world and nature are in balance. The trees, shrubbery, and grass cover the ground to keep the soil in place and provide shelter for the birds of the air and food for the animals below. Each of God's creatures from the smallest insect to the largest mammal has its place and function in God's creation. Everything worked harmoniously and in balance, and God was pleased.

Then God said, "Let us make a man, someone like ourselves, to be the master of all life upon the earth and in the skies and in the seas." So God made man like his Maker. God made man; Man and maid did he make them. Genesis 1:26-27. God controlled the animals of the kingdom by giving them certain instincts that never failed. However, God decided to give man the power to think, to make decisions and to exercise control over all that existed.

We need only to look around us to see man's creativity, imagination, inventiveness and technological skill dominating our existence. Man no longer works by the sweat of his brow. He flicks a switch or pushes a button. What used to take hours or days to accomplish is completed in minutes. Even now, the ultimate in technology is being contemplated - the cloning of man.

This is an article about harmony that begins with self, nature, home, church, worship, personal and community relationships worldwide.

Webster defines harmony as fitting together a combination of parts, a proportionate or orderly whole; congruity, agreement in feeling, action, ideas, interests, etc. peaceable or friendly relations, agreement, proportionate arrangement of color, size, shape etc. that is pleasing to the eye. An arrangement of parallel passages of different authors, the Scriptures etc. made so as to bring out corresponding ideas and qualities. Agreeable sounds, music. An excellent synonym for harmony is symmetry, similarity of form or arrangement on either side of a dividing line or plane.

There was this kind of harmony in God's creation. God intended man and nature to be in tune with each other and with the Creator. Whenever, there is a disturbance in this relationship, it is caused by man. God never changes and nature is programmed to carry on its functions, so it is man who brings disharmony. We as Christians should be mindful of this fact.

GENERAL CONFERENCE 2000

There is a lot of excitement in the air!
Methodists are assembling as the body of Christ,
On the shores of Lake Erie in Cleveland, Ohio.
They will be coming from around the globe.
As one Spirit in Christ. First General Conference of this millennium.
Bishop Jonathan Keaton: Methodist Delegates will address the issues.
Dr. Kenneth Chalker: We have covered all bases.
Dr. Julius Trimble: Be encouraged. God is with us.
Dr. Roger Skelley-Watts: Spiritual planning is the key.
Cleveland Methodists be prepared to pray and participate.
Assist where needed.

WE WHO ARE MANY ARE ONE BODY
I Corinthians 12: 1-31

The Church and the body are alike in many ways.
Just as the body must depend on each of its parts to
function well. So the Church members. though many must
be one body in love and commitment to Christ.

Without ears,
How could we hear?
Without our nose,
We couldn't smell the rose.
Without legs,
We could not walk.
Without our mouth,
We could not talk.
Without our eyes,
We could not see.

All the wonders,
On land and sea.
Created by God,
For you and me.

JESUS VISITS THE HOME OF LAZARUS, MARY AND MARTHA
September 8, 2001
John Chapter 12: 1-12

Six days before Passover would begin,
In Bethany, Jesus visited three friends.

Martha showed her love by preparing and serving,
A meal for Jesus. He was observing and deserving.

Lazarus sat at the table with smiles,
Watching the people who came from many miles,

Just to see Jesus and him, the man,
Whom Jesus raised from the dead

Mary poured fragrant oils on Jesus' feet,
While Disciple Judas watched filled with deceit.

Mary wiped Jesus' feet with her unbound hair,
The sweet fragrance filled the air.

Judas frowned on this extravagance, you know,
He wanted to be the center of the show.

He was a fund raiser and often dipped in the pot,
He did many things he should have not.

Jesus loved and blessed them all,
Mary's gift prepared him for what was to fill.

DR. JULIUS C. TRIMBLE, SENIOR PASTOR

Pastor Trimble has a powerful voice.
Yet it is commanding and soothing at the same time;
Listen carefully to the message,
You have made a wise choice.

His messages are true and strong,
By heeding them, you can do no wrong.

If you come to church sad,
His message makes you glad.

If you come to church weary,
You leave feeling cheery.

If you don't feel well,
Know that God can tell.

If you are ill,
Know that God can heal.
Pastor Trimble's sermons strengthens our hope,
And he gives us faith and courage with our problems to cope.

Frequently, he says, "I know I'm right!
We all know he has seen the light!

Minerva Primes says "He really can preach,"
And all of us know he really can teach.

Minerva says, "He is good to look at too"!
We love you, respect you and we are grateful for all you do.

REV. WILBERT TURNER, JR. ASSOCIATE PASTOR

Rev., Turner, you have been blessed with a beautiful singing voice,
You have a deep desire to study and learn God's word.
Being a preacher and a servant of God is your first choice.
In 2004 you became Associate Pastor,
You are filled with faith and hope.
Even though you are ill.
Through it all you never mope.
Rev. Turner, you are in our prayers.
You are also in God's loving care.
We pray that you will soon be home.
So that Juanita will not be alone.

THE POWER OF CHANGE

As the seasons change we adjust.
In our Heavenly Father we place our trust,
To guide us through all transitions.
We seek forgiveness for sins of omissions.
Accepting Christ is a major change,
Our way of Life is rearranged.
Everything is viewed in a different light,
For we wait on God's will and insight.
Lord, thank you for the Autumn of ninety-nine.
Our faith assures us everything will be fine.
We will enter the millennium with joy and praise,
Knowing God is with us throughout our days.

FASTING: SPIRITUAL AND PHSYCIAL RENEWAL

Matthew 6: 17-18

But when you fast, anoint your head and wash your face, that your fasting may not be seen by men but by your Father who Is in secret and your Father who sees in secret will reward you."

Matthew 4:2

This past Lenten season, I fasted 40 hours each week end from Friday mid-night until 4 P.M Sunday. I drank only water which Is purifying. I scheduled my time by praying, reading scripture, meditating and keeping a journal. I began to look forward to weekends. For me, It became a time of atonement and purification of body and spirit. Following Lent, I stopped fasting but found I missed it. Therefore, I have resumed weekend fasting. It has increased my faith, strengthened my hope and opened up new avenues of showing love not only to my family, Mends, church members but to strangers.

Prayer: Lord, thank you for sending your Son, who also fasted and prayed; suffered on the cross, triumphed over death so that all men might have everlasting life. Amen.

TRIBUTES

WRITTEN FOR THE OCCASIONOF
THE 6A GRADUATION CLASS
DANIEL E. MORGAN ELEMENTATY SCHOOL
JUNE 1960

Joy on our graduation,
It sings out in our hearts,
Yet there is sadness too,
The time has come when we must part.

Six years we've prepared too cross the stream,
We've worked hard to achieve this dream,
Future waters we will not dread
Nor the long river which waits ahead.

Since Kindergarten we have prepared
To sail our boat, not unaware that
Storms, not calm might greet us instead
As we cross the river which is ahead.

The stream is narrow,
The river is wide,
We have hopes that all of us,
Will sail on to Junior High.

Our wheel is the tool of learning,
For success we are yearning,
From the sixth grade we have tread,
The unknown river still waits ahead.

Good navigators our teachers and principal have been,
An understanding hand they would lend,
"Try again and again" they always said,
The unknown river still waits ahead.

We are now leaving shore,
We won't have to wait anymore,

We bid all a fond "good-by"
As we sail on to junior high.

Class motto: We have crossed the stream,
The river lies ahead.

WALL'S LOVE BRICKS

Making a love wall means loving all,
John Leslie Wall and Wyllene B. Wall have one loving son.
Steven Leslie Wall, Senior is a caring concerned father
A protective brick in the foundation.
Steven Leslie Wall Jr., the first brick in the foundation,
Has planned his direction,
Lord keep him focused, I pray.
Freddie, another brick we need to know,
A nurturing father in the foundation.
Ebonee Latrice, you wouldn't believe to see her now
Was born premature,
She is bright, creative, athletic, and outgoing,
A strong brick in the foundation.
Ryan is like plaster that binds,
Fast, witty and always kind,
A safe brick in the foundation
Tyler who will be thirteen in May,
Is at the stage where he loves to experiment and play
Amazingly perceptive of others moods,
He is the brick of trust in the foundation.
Taylor the Baby, ten years old,
So precious, so sweet
And Oh so spoiled!
Yet when she smiles she spreads such joy,
She is a precious brick in the Walls' foundation.

THE WALL FAMILY

FATHER'S DAY TRIBUTE TO MY HUSBAND JOHN LESLIE WALL
June 18, 1998

John believes in justice for all,
This is characteristic of a Wall.

Ongoing and outgoing in every way,
Reaching out at work or at play.

John is humorous, honest and humble,
Cheerful and happy with never a grumble.

A nurturing husband and a father so kind,
In family and music, happiness he finds.

Loyal to things he holds dear,
A husband and father without peer.

Energetic and earnest in issues worthwhile,
He manages to go through life with a smile.

Sincere and simple are his ways,
Performing his duties every day.

Loving and caring abroad and at home,
He is never one to wander or roam.

Interested in the, "Vision Choir."
His commitment is one that does inspire.

Every man should be so blest,
To pass the Father's Day Test.

Willing to give and forgive,
What a wonderful way to live!

All for one and one for all
Is the motto of John Wall.

Loving, listening, and learning,
Happy Fathers Day, honey!

FATHER'S DAY
June 3, 1998

A father is a role model for his children and for other children as well. The way he lives his life is the lesson his children learn.

- **F** Foster a faith for them to follow all their lives.
- **A** Actions teach them more than words.
- **T** Teach them tenderness so they grow in compassion.
- **H** Humbleness and honesty are heavenly values.
- **E** Every job should be completed to the best of their ability.
- **R** Respect for themselves and others Resourcefulness.

FOR STEVE'S 39TH BIRTHDAY
June 29, 1998

Birthdays are special.
They come but once a year,
Enjoy your 39th!
Celebrate with family and friends both far and near.

Let your hair down,
Put your feet up,
Relax with kids around,
Let joy and happiness fill your cup.

Pause for a moment,
Reflect on 39 years of living,
What is most dear to you?
Praise and thank God for the giving.

A TRIBUTE TO STEVEN L. WALL
June 30, 2007

Steve is handsome and debonair,
He is trustworthy and kind,
Generous and willing to share
All he possesses even his time and his mind.

He is talented and can fix anything,
All the while working and laughing,
All the while singing and joking,
For all his work, he will accept only a token.

He may not be in church every Sunday,
But he keeps in touch with God, reading and praying
Each morning before he starts his day;
Each night, before he goes to sleep, he asks God to show him the way.

He teaches his children in subtle ways,
Ready to listen filled with praise,
Always patient and pleasant,
He explains what is in his heart and what is on his mind.

Steve is a loving, thoughtful son,
Willing to help in every way,
Through it all, he is full of play,
This kind of love and joy he brings to each new day.

Your Dad and I love you, Steve,
You and your children are our pride and joy.
Dad and I pray for you,
Our only son and child!

When we have to leave you here,
Live you life without fear,

We know you are in God's hands,
And that we will meet again in that heavenly land.

Love, Mom

TAYLOR'S TENTH BIRTHDAY
April 2, 2008

Taylor, you are ten years old today,
Hope you will be happy in every way.
Open your gifts and say "thank you"
As you grow older remain sweet, pure and true.

I only see you every other week,
Things would be different if we would speak,
A little more often or better every day,
We could keep in touch until your weekend stay.

The WALL FAMILY wishes you a HAPPY BIRTHDAY!
As you celebrate your tenth year in joyous fun and play.
Rejoice in it every way you can
That is how your birthday was planned.

TYLER'S 13TH BIRTHDDAY

Tyler, you've become a teenager today!
Grandma's special baby boy,
As you grow and develop in every way
You are full of surprises and a bundle of joy.

Keep smiling, keep learning
As you grow taller each day,
Know for what you are yearning,
Articulate what you want to say.

Enjoy your first teenage year,
Study and learn all you can,

There is nothing in life you need to fear
Someday, you will become a brilliant man!

HAVE A JOYFUL 13TH BIRTHDAY
BE THANKFUL FOR ALL THAT COMES YOUR WAY!

40TH WEDDING ANNIVERSARY
CHARLES AND ESTHER ENGLISH
JUNE 18, 1996

Forty Years In Any Endeavor Is A Milestone.
Forty Years Of Successful Participation In Any Endeavor Is A Monumental Achievement!
Forty Years Of A Happy Marriage Is Significant And Rare.

We are gathered here to share in this special occasion for Charles and Esther English- their 40th Wedding Anniversary- a marvelous celebration of their life together.

There have been highs and lows in their lives,
Periods of sorrow, sickness and strife,
Through it all, they have remained together,
Closer together, if that is possible.

During the years, there may have been
A few broken promises, some disagreements,
A shattered dream or two and maybe some regrets,
Through it all they stayed together, 40 years of success.

They learned to compromise and communicate,
They showed compassion and love for each other,
They cherished the values of their fathers and mothers,
They respected their vows and held on to their faith.

Charles and Esther are a couple to admire, emulate and congratulate!

The high times have been many:
The birth of Collete,
Her growing up years,
Her graduation,
And a successful career,
Marriage to Douglas, gave them a son.

Finally Kelsey, a granddaughter to spoil and enjoy.
Esther's B.S. and M.A. degrees,
Building their dream home was a breeze.
Esther's retirement,
A second career, instructor at Tri-C,
A community volunteer.

Both share a deep church involvement and strong religious faith, which has never wavered through all the quirks and turns of fate. Charles and Esther both enjoy travel, and have done so extensively in the United States, Canada, Europe, China and Hawaii. They have been on eleven romantic cruises, actually twelve, if we count the one where Esther was ill the entire time. They will be flying to Bermuda on July 11, their 4th trip there. Each year, the Englishes and the Dixons vacation together at Hilton Head S.C.

About the lows in their lives, just recently they lost Charles' brother who suffered a long illness, Esther's mother had a stroke and Elaine, their sister-in-law is recovering from one. Into every life some rain must fall. Charles and Esther believe it pays to carry the right umbrella. For them it is their trust in God!

This is a couple who is compatible in many ways, even in the letters of their names.

C	Courageous and Courteous
H	Honest and Humble
A	Ambitious and Amiable
R	Religious and Reliable
L	Loyal and a Leader
S	Systematic and Sincere
E	Elegant and Exciting
S	Scholarly and Sympathetic

T	Truthful and Trustworthy
H	Hopeful and Helpful
E	Enthusiastic and Engaging
R	Reverent and Resourceful
E	Entertaining
N	Nurturing
G	Generous
L	Loving
I	Imaginative
S	Stable
H	Hospitable Host and Hostess

50TH ANNIVERSARY JESSE AND RICHARDEAN COVINGTON
May 25, 1996

Fifty years, you've been together,
Together, you've made each year better,
Married in 1946, the eighth of June,
You've had one long honeymoon.

I can see Jesse full of pride,
The day he came to claim his bride,
A young and willing Richardean,
Soon to become Jesse's queen.

You both worked hard and bought a home,
A place from which you would seldom roam,
Except for visits to parents, relatives and friends,
This was the love that gave you wings.

Jesse and Richardean, how you loved the Lord,
You joined the church with one accord,
Each giving service in your special way,
Thanking God for his goodness every day.

With parents and old friends gone,
You decided to visit Rome,
You call this period the "traveling years,"
You circled the globe without any fears.

Romantic cruises to Nassau and Freeport,
Many trips to a show in New York,
California, Arizona and Washington D.C.
Let us not forget the trip to Hawaii!

Daytona Beach, Florida under the sun,
The Kentucky Derby to see the horses run,

Israel, a magic faraway land,
Philadelphia, St. Louis, Cincinnati, Assemblies, grand.

You promised as husband and wife,
To live together all your life,

To comfort each other in sickness or health,
To share the hard times as well as the wealth.

Congratulations to a fifty year couple,
May your blessings and love be doubled,
We gathered here to wish you well,
In God and happiness, continue to dwell.

BISHOP JULIUS CALVIN TRIMBLE

B	Beloved husband, father, pastor, teacher and friend
I	Inspirational speaker
S	Sincere and secure in his beliefs
H	Humorous, hopeful, humble and helpful
O	Obedient, outspoken, outgoing and outstanding
P	Preaches the word and praises the Lord.
J	Jesus Christ is his anchor and role model
U	Upright and understanding
L	Loving, excellent listener
I	Interesting, intellectual
U	Has urgent goals
S	Sensitive, sound wisdom
C	Comforting and caring
A	Aggressive
L	Loyal
V	Victorious
I	Involved in all areas of the church
N	Nurturing to all he meets,
T	Trustworthy,
R	Respectful and respected
I	Imaginative, interesting, instinctively knows what to do
M	He is on God's Mission
B	He is a blessing to all who know him
L	Liberal and lively
E	May every thing you do and everywhere you go be blessed by God.

TOM SKINNER

T   Trust worthy scholar gifted with theological thoughts,
Tom is true to the theories the Bible has taught.

O   Omnipotent God, you are his master,
You save him and us from all disaster.

M   Missions he supports and God's message preaches,
Attends meetings and in workshops teaches.

S   Sermons and singing he praises his Savior,
In His vineyard he is willing to labor.

K   Knowledge he is always willing to share,
And the knack to kindle hearts to care.

I   Instructor, interpreter, inspirer, he is,
Interested in all things concerning his peers.

N   Nurturing the notion to use nature's gifts,
Now and forever, God's beauty uplifts.

N   Nearer to newness, nearer to thee,
Never more safe, yet never more free.

E   Everlasting to everlasting he believes,
His eternal evangelism he perceives.

R   Reverent revivals, rhetoric profound,
Revealing through Christ the way that is sound.

TRIBUTE TO REV. H. WALTER WILLIS

H	He is honest, honorable, yet humble,
W	Willing to serve, wise and witty,
A	Amiable, astute able, articulate.
L	Loyal, loveable, a leader of people,
T	Thoughtful, trustworthy, trusts in God.
E	Energetic, enthusiastic with an ebullient spirit,
R	Reverent, reliable, responsible, in all respects.
W	He has wonderful words, worthy words of wisdom.
I	Inspiring sermons, Christian ideals imbued with intellectual integrity.
L	He is always ready to listen, willing to learn and longing to cure the ills of the world.
L	Ever looking for lasting ways to lessen sin and sorrow,
I	He is an influential instructor with ingenious innovations,
S	A super speaker and gifted singer are the sundry words with which we describe our Pastor- with love.

TRIBUTE TO REV. RAYMOND BURGESS
July 23, 1977

You came,
You saw, you had work to do
Teaching and preaching
And building a Church too.

Births, baptisms, weddings,
Funerals, the gamut you have shared,
Christenings, vows,
And your consoling cares.

You came,
You saw, outreaching was your way,
Serving the whole man
By night as well as day.

You came,
You saw membership steadily grow,
Love, hope and faith,
You wanted the church to know.

All this we will treasure,
When you depart,
A pastor without measure,
Rev. Burgess, you are dear to our hearts.

This card was made,
So you would know,
How much we hate,
To see you go.

EVELYN GOODSON

Evelyn, you are energetic, vivacious, loving, elegant in dress and speech. You say, "yes" to most requests and you are nurturing.

Evelyn, you created a ministry
from a secretarial role,
you've respected and helped
the timid and the bold.

When we joined Aldersgate,
you inspired us with hope.
You were kind and patient
and taught us the ropes.

You are a walking encyclopedia
on Aldersgate and the United Methodist Church.

We will miss
your smiling face
and your expertise.

Aldersgate, your warmhearted family
wishes you all the benefits of retirement:
sleeping late,
travel and
doing what you never had time for before.

ALDERSGATE UMC CELEBRATES

Aldersgate UMC celebrated the retirement of Evelyn Odean Maples Goodson,

January 25, 03 at the Warrensville Civic/Senior Center at 5 P.M

Evelyn has served as Administrative Secretary for over twenty years. Willie Mae Ewings-Travis, Mistress of Ceremony who also presented the Proclamation/ Resolutions. Welcome by Rev. Benita Rollins. Benevolence, Rosalyn Grant. Musical selections by The Quintet Plus One. Reflections, from former Pastors: Rosa Clements, James Thomas and Maurice King. Reflections by Church member Harold Gilmore. Reflections by Melanie Goodson, daughter. The theme was "A Virtuous Woman," based on Proverbs 31:10-31.

"Who can find a Virtuous Woman? For her price is far above rubies." "Her children rise up and call her blessed…"

"She stretcheth out her hand to the poor,…" …a woman that feareth the

Lord, she shall be praised."

Evelyn left a few days later for a trip to Rome.

DORIS AND EDDIE FIELDS: 50ᵀᴴ WEDDING ANNIVERSARY
August 10, 2003

D	Doris, a demure, devoted, distinctive blushing bride,
O	On the threshold to wed Eddie, who was bursting with pride.
R	Respected and revered by all of her peers.
I	In marrying Eddie she had no fears.
S	So today, they celebrate fifty years of wedded bliss.
A	An admirable and adorable team.
N	Nothing has ever shattered their love,
D	Determined to hold on to their dream.
E	Eddie, ever eager to please Doris, his wife.
D	Devoted to her and their children for life.
D	Demanding, is Eddie in ways that really matter.
I	Instilling integrity in their beautiful daughters, Debra and Shirra
E	Extra instruction and love for son-in-law Charles, grand children Charles Jr., Nicole, Mikko, Charlotte, Allie and Alden.
F	Fortunate are the Fields to celebrate fifty fabulous years and Fantastic memories and events too numerous to count.
I	In Christ the Fields put their trust,
E	Embarking on new missions is a must.
L	Loyal supporters of peace and justice.
D	Daring to reach out to others who are in need,
S	Sincere and sympathetic in spreading their deeds.

May God Continue to bless you with contentment and longevity. You are both role models for others.

CONDOLENCES
June 15, 1998

When your heart is broken, it's all right to cry,
When you are fearful, it is time to pray,
The Lord hears your every sigh,
He is with you night and day.

As long as you can remember,
All the good times you shared together,
As long as you remember, the bright and stormy weather,
As long as you remember, _____ is with you always.

DEATH OF A CLOSE FRIEND

To lose a _____
Brings so much grief,
It is a pain hard to bear,
Yet God offers this relief,
I am with you always
I will give you peace.

May it help you to know
Your friends at READ
Share your pain
And extend their deepest sympathy.

REFLECTIONS ON DEATH

Someone asked, "What is death?
When the hearts stops beating,
The voice is stilled,
The eyes closed
The body cold?"

"I know," someone answered,
The soul wings it way
To a heavenly resting place,
After its earthly stay."

"What of the dead?"
The mourners asked,
From some higher plane,
Do they see the grief,
The shock, the despair,
Their leaving have wrought?"

"My child, the faithful replied,
We know that God cares.
His assurance of a new birth
In Christ is there."

Weep not for the departed,
Rather, comfort the living,
Seek God' solace and mercy,
Let your life be one of giving.

Through death we enter
A new life, a spiritual one,
Promised by our Father's Son,
Jesus Christ, our Lord
If the departed died believing in Him.

REST IN PEACE - FRED SPANN
October 5, 1969

Your sunny smile never revealed
The torment seething inside,
Your quick quips always concealed
Inner problems you would hide.

In some dark echo of your mind
Life lost its meaning,
You sought at last to find
A release from troubled dreaming.

I will always remember your kindness,
The last conversation we shared,
Never detecting in my blindness,
That in you lurked despair!

Our Maker in his mercy will understand,
Where you friends can never be sure,
What fierce forces made such a demand?
That life you could no longer endure.

Dear friend, rest in peace,
Although your loved ones are left forlorn,
Their love for you will never cease,
Even when hearts are troubled and torn.

The one who watches over all,
Will comfort them day by day,
To accept your desperate call,
May you rest in peace, we pray.

A TRIBUTE TO MY COUSIN, JOHNNIE MARY BROWN

Johnnie, remember when we tried to give each other what we called "nick" names. You wanted to be called "Joy" and I chose "Billie." You often called me "Bill" but although "Joy" didn't catch on as a name, you were a joy to me and all who knew you. You had such a vital, interesting personality. I am going to miss you, girl! When Bob called me and told me, a light was dimmed for me. But I feel confident that your light is shining on the other side and that it is brighter over there.

Johnnie, remember the picture of the three of us, you, Mary Elizabeth and me. I am looking at the picture now. We have on dresses with full skirts down to our ankles. All three of us are smiling. This was taken during one of Mary's trips here. We all have April birthdays: yours on the 16th, Mary's on the 12th and mine on the 5th. We were always discussing how alike we were and how different we were. We are only children of two brothers and a sister. You were a devoted and loyal daughter to Auntie, She loved you dearly. I am thinking about all the good times we shared. Auntie used to cook dinner on Thanksgiving with all the trimmings and a big pot of "Chitterlings." Remember Sam, who said no he didn't eat them but once he tasted Auntie's, he couldn't get enough. Those backyards picnics you had were such fun and the food was delicious. I'll always remember your birthday parties at the Trophy Lounge. You were always consoling and a comfort to me when there were troubles in my life. You were there for me to talk to and sort things out. I always admired your attitude. You would never let any thing get you down. You would always find the bright side.

You were a loyal and true friend which is evidenced by the calls I get almost daily from the friends you have in Cleveland asking about you and praying for you.

Johnnie, you were a good mother to Gwen and Robert and grandmother to Robert Jr. God will take care of Robert and Robert Jr. You were a very helpful mother-in-law to Barbara. In all respects, you have had a very full life. You have played an important role in the lives of all the people who have known you, family as well as friends. You were never afraid to show love. You so willingly shared with those less fortunate than you. You often thought of my church, St. Paul United Methodist Church and sent donations to the Church and Sunday School.

Johnnie, I am going to miss you but I shall keep alive loving memories of you until I join you and other loved ones in The Great Beyond. I will remember you as you were in June 1992 when John and I were there.

Robert, let not your heart be troubled: Jesus said "Ye believe in God believe also in me." He will take care of you and sustain you during this dark hour of grief. I wish I could be there with you, but I am there in spirit.

Sleep on Johnnie and take your rest; lay down your head on Jesus' breast!

SPRING SAFETY AND IN MEMORY OF WILLIAM BETT'S FATHER
MARCH 1976

Let me play and have some fun,
As I enjoy the bright spring sun,
I will remember as I play,
To practice safety every day.

When he left me all alone,
My heart was filled with grief,
In loving arms, he went home,
In my faith is this belief.

He lives on in each of us.
In memories ever clear,
His strength, his will, his care,
Keeps his presence always near.

Someday when I journey home,
I will see him face to face,
When I look into his eyes,
I will know I have won the race.

FUNERAL FOR MARIAN JACKSON DOWNS

M	Marriage a happy one
A	Activities she never shunned
R	Righteous, she was that too
I	Inspiration she spread like dew
A	Answering the call of need
N	Neighborly in doing a deed

J	Being just and jolly as well
A	Anxieties she could dispel
C	Courage never wavered
K	Kindness and special favors
S	Serene in the midst of storms
O	Opinions given calmly
N	Nearness to God's light

D	Doing always what was right
O	Owing no sister or brother
W	Wife, like her no other
N	Noting now, her life is free
S	She has already earned her key.

TRIBUTE TO MRS. BESSIE PORTER

It is true, we lose this life,
It is the price we pay,
To gain the promised resurrection,
In mansions Jesus has prepared for us to stay,
When we arise triumphant over death.
As I closed my weary eyes,
To embrace my final,
Inescapable sleep.
It was like a dream,
The dark walls
which surrounded me,
Began to crumble and fall.
I could see behind,
Over, around and beyond.
I remembered my past,
It was as if my whole
Life flashed before me,
Visions of my parents,
My husband, my children
other relatives and friends,
So real, I could see.
I could also feel
And see the welcoming
Future stretching out before me.
I realized how safe
I would be there, with Jesus,
To abide in everlasting
love and peace.
As I was crossing over,
I felt a deep penetrating sense of freedom,
A wonderful release of body and soul,

Dear ones, I will wait to greet you
When your time comes to enter the fold.

IN MEMORY OF MR. JOHN POWELL
June 9, 1995

My husband, (who is also named) John and I have known Mr. John T. Powell for a decade.

He taught my sister-in-law, Dorothy Wall, who has since moved to Fresno California. He started my grandson, 6 year old Steve Jr., my nephew, Billie and me on the piano. He has really touched the lives of the Wall family. I've taken the letter of his name to help explain the influence he has made not only in our lives but also as a choir director and organist of Liberty Hill Baptist Church and music teacher and role model for many students.

J   He was jovial and jolly, no matter what crisis he was experiencing

O   He was an organist of stellar dimensions, yet he told me he always practiced on Thursdays for about 2 hours.

H   He is handsome, always dressed in suit, tie with everything coordinated from head to toe. He has a keen sense of humor also.

N   He was blessed with a natural musical gift and love of music, which he elevated to his highest potential.

T   He was a thoughtful person, a thinker, teacher and tutor.

P   He was persistent in his expectations. He expects his students to practice and practice. He is the Perfect Pianist.

O	He was orderly in his teaching techniques, the wrist up just so, correct fingering and proper way to strike the key, wrist and arm movements, rhythm and time. He stressed short fingernails.
W	He worshiped God with his whole heart and expressed it through word and music.
E	He was an enthusiastic teacher always encouraging and eager to impart knowledge.
L	He was loyal and dedicated to his family, art, church, proud of his heritage.
L	He had limitless patience in teaching students and with his choir, He was a lover of music.

IN MEMORY WILLA JESSMA PERCIVAL
April 28, 2006

Let me begin by extending my sympathy to Maury and his wife, Marion, Ann and the rest of the family. In Matt 5:14, the scripture reads, Blessed are they that mourn for they shall be comforted. All of us are in a state of mourning right now! May our Lord, Jesus Christ who gave us everlasting comfort and good hope, comfort your hearts and give you strength in every good thing you do and say. God's Word is as close as our fingertips and God himself is as close as our whispered prayer. Know that your mother, your sister, your grandmother, your aunt, your cousin and your friend has run her race and is now in heaven where she has earned her place.

Willa's life was that of a true Christian from early childhood until God called her home on Monday April 17, 2006.

Willa was my true friend from beginning to the end. God blessed her with many gifts: a beautiful singing voice, an excellent pianist, an interesting speaker, a prolific reader, well educated, a caring nursing profession, blessed with two talented sons, a friendly and outgoing personality, strong and independent, courageous, always willing to help. She used all these talents throughout her life. Willa, I am going to miss our long conversations and discussions.

Thank you for bringing sunshine
To my gray and glooming days,
For being there when needed,
And for your caring, loving ways.
Thank you for encouragement
When I was weary and distraught,
For words of consolation,
And for all the joy you brought.

Thank you for all your prayers
That were made on my behalf,
For helping to erase my tears
And to replace them with a laugh.
I can face each new tomorrow,
For I know I can depend...
On God...who sent an angel,
And it is you...My precious friend.

MY SPECIAL POEMS, PHILOSOPHY & WORDS

A DAY IN JANUARY
January 12, 1955

May I come in for a moment
As Ted Malone would say
Although you may be sad
It is a lovely day.

The snow is falling
Without a sound
It's so soft and white
Why do you frown?

Pause in your work
Or in your play
Watch each flake so tiny and light
The snow it makes.

Oh, lovely snow
Are you here to stay
To cover the trees
With a brilliant spray?

To paint the house tops
All in white
And deck the lawns
With a radiant light?

What artist
To paint such?
There is magic
In all you touch.

SEASONAL THOUGHTS
1969

The changing of the seasons
Always bring nostalgic longings
About things that have passed;
Yet a hopeful yearning
For the things worth learning.

****

In the long and lonely night,
My heart searched for an answer,
In the sad, sleepless night
My thoughts were troubled,
I prayed for God's insight.

MATHEMATICS CONSULTANTS

From a shaky expectation
To a certain calculation.

Remediation is our job,
Find the effective way,
Helping children to absorb
More concepts each day.

Hyman, Blount and Whiting,
All the VIP'S were there,
Ideas flowed like lighting
Your thoughts you would share.

WORKSHOP MATHEMATICS 1970

Multi base blocks
Red and green pieces,
Make us take stock
Of consultant's leases.

We learned adding and subtraction,
Worked with negative numbers
We decided why fractions
Caused so many blunders.

Mathematics is an exciting game,
As you strive to teach
Many digits you rename,
And finally a solution reaches.

Our workshops are complete
There is always something new
To evaluate and give reports too

****

I feel so much better when I write
What is on my mind like I did tonight?

I am happier when I let my thoughts flow
My emotions, desires all seem to show.

****

When I awake at night,
And the house is still
I listen to the silence
What things I hear!

INTROSPECTION JUNE 1969

The southern spring day ended at last,
The soft shade of dusk descended fast,
My thoughts are filled with memories of my youth
When life was simple and filled with truth.

The Alabama sun disappeared from sight,
As I stood without fear in the twilight.
The scent of honey suckles filled the air,
Intoxicatingly sweet on an evening so fair.

When I closed my eyes, I could see and hear,
A cowbell sounding, Oh so near!
Fireflies flashing in the dark,
The sweet song of a meadow lark.

A child again swinging on the gate,
Swinging, swaying until it is late,
The scene seems so serene and real,
A child again is how I feel!

THE FAMILY TOGETHER
May 10, 1982

T	The family together in a place
H	Called home, where growing and nurturing
E	Experiences surface and are faced.

F	For fathers and Grandfathers
A	Aunts, and Uncles
M	Mothers and Grandmothers, cousins
I	Important family members, everyone.
L	Love for children, each daughter and son
Y	Yielding their lives to the will of God.

T	Thankful, thoughtful and truthful
O	Outgoing, ongoing which is prime,
G	Graciously giving at all times.
E	Encouraging, enjoying, companionship families share,
T	Trusting and loving God and then have love to spare,
H	Home is the Family together!
E	Embracing Christ's love in all kinds of weather,
R	Religion and respect are the reasons, families live better.

PERFECTLY GRAND

Grandmama, you are grand,
I like it when you hold my hand,
As we cross a busy street,
To McDonald's for a treat.

Grandmama, you are very wise,
I like to have you by my side,
As we stroll through the mall,
I am small but you are tall.

Grandmama, you are lots of fun,
You play games and you can run,
You and Grandpa take us for rides,
Sight seeing and playing on slides.

Grandmama, we have time for talks,
In the afternoon, we take our walks,
We watch TV and read our book,
Still have time to help you cook.

A CHILD'S TRUST

Grand Mama is what Tyler calls me,
All the other children say Grand ma,
Steve Jr. Ebonee', Ryan and Taylor.
They all love Jesus Christ, our Savior.

"Grand mama, what is the millennium?
Asked Tyler, who is four,
A word he keeps hearing,
More and more.

Grand mama started to explain
As best she could
To allay his fears
As a grand ma should,

"Grand mama, "Tyler, interrupted,
Don't worry about it.
God will take care of us and
If he doesn't, my Daddy will!"

CHRIST MAKES US ONE

United Methodists, one community of faith,
Comprised of every race under the sun,
Brown, yellow, black, white and red,
Through all cultures, Jesus' name is spread.

In all ways that count, we are united
As one body, we worship Jesus Christ.
Through love of God and love of man,
Our commitment and faith go hand and hand.

Methodism is known in every land,
Missionaries have traveled south, north, east and west.

Building schools, churches, hospitals and playgrounds.
Teaching love, health, caring and all the rest.

ODE TO AFRICAN-AMERICAN WOMEN

Beautiful, ebony to coffee cream,
Mystical, African-American woman,
Stolen from her native home
Brilliant, brave of heart
In history, she played her part and left her mark.

She is a mother, gentle but firm,
Or she has assumed the role of mother,
This caring African-American woman
Nurturing, not only her own but other youths,
In high moral values and spiritual truths.

She is an educator, loyal and dedicated,
This intelligent African-American woman,
She teaches and shares her knowledge,
"Be prepared, is her advice, what ever
Career you choose, what is learned you can't lose."

She is a Christian, faithful and true,
This devoted devout African-American woman,
Prayer and hope are measuring rods
She looks for good, expects the best,
Stands ready with God to meet any test.

She is a role model, with beauty and brains,
A trail blazer this African American woman,
A fore runner, she rises to new heights,
Sharing and caring are her goals in life,
She knows first hand how to deal with strife.

She is a pioneer, exploring and searching
This inquisitive African-American woman,
She breaks down barriers,
Unafraid of the future, aware of the past.
She knows the fight for justice is an awesome task.

She is uncompromising in her quests
This demanding, African-American woman,

She refuses to accept," can't," I can't, you can't
they can't, we can't; neither has she accepted, "no."
Persistent and pursuing she has opened many a door.

She is a survivor, righteous and courageous,
This fearless phenomenal African-American woman,
She inherited the trials of slavery,
She has traveled a long rough road,
Tried, tired, undaunted, willing to shoulder the load.

Mystical African-American women, beautiful, ebony to coffee cream,
You have kept the faith and fostered the dream
Bright, productive, progressive, resilient, sensitive and talented,
These daughters of former slaves are challengers, doers' motivators and movers.
They are articulate, prepared and proud, beautiful, ebony to coffee cream,
Mystical African American Women.

ODE TO LOVE

Love consumes like flames from a raging fire,
Unleashed then dies down to smoldering embers.
Love is a bag of mixed emotions and memories,
Love is a combination of happiness and pain,
Love is forgiving again and again

Love is fascination, like smoke and rain,
Smoke that rolls thick and fast,
Then fades to a thin grey mist.
Rain falling in torrents, wild and strong,
Then become a gentle rhymic beat like a song.

Love is still love in its passion or tranquility,
Is the sea less dangerous, because its waves are calm?
How swiftly can the sky darken though now it is blue?
The wind is not measured by the breeze now blowing,
Love is still love through its changing and growing.

Published in "BEST POEMS OF 1997," The National Library of Poetry. Howard Ely, Editor.

THE WORLD NEEDS LOVE

What the world need is to spread love around,
Then love has the power to keep us sound.

Love can lift us, up when our burden is heavy,
It can keep our faith steadfast and steady.

Let us freely give as well as accept love,
We need to love each other as the little dove.

We need to expect love as if it is our right,
No questions, no doubts, bask in the beam of its light.

The world needs to accept love in all its forms and races,
The world needs to share love, in all times and places.

GRADUATION

Boys and girls in schools,
All over the land to day,
Are receiving their diplomas,
In their faces, one sees hope,
The unafraid optimism of the young,
We pray they will follow their dream,
No matter how difficult the going may seem.

The black boy and the girl
As they enter the battle for employment,
Not only will an energy crisis face,
But discrimination against their race.
They must keep their courage steady,
The banner of equality raises high,
They will surely reach the top,
By never letting persistence stop.

Life for them holds a challenge,
They venture forth to meet,
Success, mediocrity or defeat,
Fear not the sweat of brow,
Fear not the lash of scorn,
You have faced some kind of trouble
Since the day you were born.

Your heritage is one of slavery,
Of it be not ashamed,
Your hearts and souls are free,
Some day you will earn your fame.
You have heard the word democracy,
Throughout your short life span,
With it reach a successful plan.

You ask why democracy,
When applied to a black person's life,
Fails in its noble sounding phrases,
And you face discrimination and strife,

Blacks must fight for their future,
And for their children's too,
The reality of freedom is waiting just for you.

PREPARATION
Summer 1963

Busy little ant,
Busy as can be,
Wither take that large crumb
To store away until winter comes?

Busy little ant,
Toil all summer long,
You will rest in your snug hole,
When winter comes and the wind blows cold.

IF

If you've never felt lonely,
In a crowd,
If you've never shed a tear,
Because you are proud,
Then you've never been sad.

If you've never felt blue,
While the music played,
If you've never felt guilty
When your thoughts have strayed,
Then you've never been sad.

If you've never had a longing,
That wasn't right,
If you've never shed a tear,
In the still of the night,
Then you've never been sad.

If you've known love,
Though now it is gone,
If your heart hasn't been left

Bleeding and torn,
Then you've never been sad.

I USE TO
July 1975

I used to attend church every Sunday,
I use to be very active,
I used to be involved in everything,
Now I am tired, I don't have the time,
But I used to do, you say,
But it's not what you used to do that counts,
It's what you do today.

I use to teach Sunday School,
But now I need my rest,
I use to sing in the choir,
I used to do my very best,
I use to do you say,
It's not what you used to do that counts,
It's what you do today.

I use to help in every way,
But now I don't have the time, you say,
I use to me at every call,
Now it's some other time or not at all,
I use to do, you say,
It's not what you used to do that counts,
It's what you do today.

Suppose we had a use to do God,
Who was tired or didn't have the time?
Who said when we needed him,
I must rest, or ask somebody else,
He is doing the same thing now,
It's not what you used to do, that counts,
It's what you do today.

BLACK ACHIEVEMENT
1976

B   Beauty, brawn and brains,
L   A long life of learning
A   Active, ambitions, aims
C   Courageous, Church going Christians
K   Keeping kin and kindness

A   Ability, awareness, working in accord
C   Christ's compassion and care
H   Honesty, humor and hope
I   Interest, empathy, and inspiration
E   Eternal endurance and endeavor
V   Variety, vigor and virtue
E   Emulation of every essential effort
M   Mature decisions
E   Efforts of all blacks are essential
N   Nurture of nature and notions
T   Temples, temperance and tasks

RHYMED COUPLETS – ON COUNSELING
May 9, 1976

Counseling is a way children grow,
With an effective counselor this growth will show.

Counseling is a special way,
To insure progress in this day.

Keep trying methods until you find the way,
To solve educational problems we face today.

A counselor should have a special skill,
To motivate students when it's against their will.

THANK YOU CARD FROM THE READING CLINIC
June 1, 1976

Thank you for the exquisite milk glass vase,
Here at home we will always enjoy your taste,
Artistically arranged where it will glow,
Nothing could have pleased us more, you know,
Keeping your well wishes in mind,
We say, "thank you" for being so kind.

RIDING YOUR BIKE
Spring 1977

Ride your bike,
You have the right,
But always wear
White at night.

Ride your bike,
After school,
But always obey
The safety rules.

Ride your bike,
Enjoy your ride,
"Don't try to "show off,"
Keep the law on your side.

HIGH COST OF LOVING

"You don't love me! How may times have your kids laid that one on you? And how many times have you as a parent, resisted the urge to tell them how much? Someday,

When my children are old enough to understand that motivates a mother, I'll tell them.

I loved you enough to bug you about where you were going, with whom and what time you would be home

I loved you enough to insist you buy a bike with your money that we could afford and you could not.

I loved you enough to be silent and let you discover your hand picked friend was a creep.

I loved you enough to make you return a Milky Way with a bite out of it to a drug store and confess, "I stole this."

I loved you enough to stand over you for two hours while you cleaned your bedroom, a job that would have taken me 15 minutes.

I loved you enough to say you could go to Disney World on Mother's Day.

I loved you enough to let you see anger, disappointment, disgust and tears in my eyes.

I loved you enough to not let you make excuses for your lack of respect or your bad manners.

I loved you enough to admit I was wrong and ask your forgiveness.

I loved you enough to ignore "what every other mother "did or said.

I loved you enough to let you stumble, fall, hurt and fail.

I loved you enough to let you assume the responsibility for your own actions at 6, 10, 16.

I loved you enough to figure you would lie about the party being chaperoned, but

forgave you for it after discovering I was right.

I loved you enough to shove you off my lap, let go of your hand be mute to your pleas and insensitive to your demands so that you could stand alone.

I loved you enough to accept you for what you are, not what I wanted you to be. But most of all I loved you enough to say "No", when you hated me for it. That was the hardest part of all.

ADVICE FOR PARENTS

Parents, this is food for thought, think about the following advice that I have found to be sound in helping my son to grow into the kind of loving, thoughtful and successful man he is today. I am so proud of his loving care for his dad and me. For his help, advise and respect. No one could wish for a better son.

Too often parents are able to afford many nice things in life and they simply share them with their children without teaching them to earn the "nice things." Let them earn the "good life" through learning responsibility.

Middle school children can certainly take out garbage; clean the basement and garage weekly. Help shovel snow in the winter. Help care for the lawn in the spring and summer. Learn how to vacuum the carpet, set the table and etc. Naturally, you are expected to give them an allowance, part of which they spend and part of which they are taught to save by opening a bank account in their name.

When they reach High School age, even more can be expected of them. They can begin to earn their own spending money.

Often when students see their peers with nice things and money, they feel cheated by their own parents. Later, they will realize this is not the case. Their parents are simply trying to teach them that nice things are appreciated more when earned.

In the late teens, youngsters finally begin to realize what their parents have been trying to teach them. All children should earn their allowance and their fine home.

The best gift that parents can instill is one of responsibility.

SPRING
March 23, 1977

S   Is for the signs of spring,
         Wind so soft and birds that sing.

P   Is for plowing the hard earth,
         And all things begin a new birth.

R   Is for the relieving shower,
         That quenches the thirst of every flower.

I   Is for instant beauty and fun,
         Inspiring sights under the sun.

N   Is for nature all around,
         It seems like magic, it is so profound.

G   Is for the gay, good times together,
         No other time is like spring weather.

W   Is for winter, the time we go,
         Trudging to school through the snow.

I   Is for icicles that clutch and cling,
         To the trees as the north wind sings.

N   Is for noon, the hour of the day,
         We stop to eat and sometimes play.

T   Is teachers who are kind,
         They insist we learn and make us mind.

E   Is for effort, we do out best,
         We find we can pass any test.

R   Is for weather rugged and rough,
     The kind of weather that makes us tough.

MY DAD
MAY 1977

My Dad is a quiet man,
Always doing the best he can,
Yet, I know he is always there,
Willing and ready to do his share.

My Dad is a happy man,
Laughing and joking whenever he can,
Yet, a problem he never side steps,
He tackles head on and truly helps.

My Dad corrects me when I am wrong,
His rules are few but very strong,
When he disciplines, he doesn't play,
His training has helped me in every way.

My Dad will be a hard man to follow,
With more like him, there would be less sorrow,
My Dad believes in the "Golden Rule,"
"Do unto others as you would have them do to you."

This poem is dedicated to your Dad and mine,
No better fathers will you ever find.
We love you and thank you too,
For all the thoughtful things you do.

Remember this Dad, wherever I roam,
Thank you for a Christian home.
I can never forget my religious up bringing,
Stay close to God and continue singing.

KNOW YOURSELF
February 1995

How do you feel at the end of the day?
Frustrated, Happy, Angry?

Were the hours filled with useful work
Or were they empty and sad?
Ask yourself, "Why am I frustrated?"
"What went wrong?"
"Did I ask for help to face the day
From the Creator above?"
"Did I prepare myself adequately
Seeking God's help along the way?"

Ask yourself, "why am I happy?"
"Did I start the day with God?"
"So he could help me do the job?"
"Did I keep negative thoughts and
Influences at bay?"
"Is that why I am so happy today?"

Ask yourself, "Why am I angry?"
"Did I try to do the work alone?"
"Was I efficient and sufficient on my own?"
"Then why am I angry?"
"Am I angry at myself?"
"To whom or what is my anger directed?"
Lord, help me!
Take away this hard core of anger.

I will pray each day,
Avoid negatives,
I will be happy with myself.

THE TRAGEDY OF SUSAN SMITH

What pushed a mother over the edge?
The demons, in her distraught mind, who knows?
How could this happen today?
A young mother, alone and lonely,
Remembering failed dreams,
Holding inside silent screams, who knows?
The crime so heinous and bold,
Formed in a mind grown cold,
Numb with unbearable suffering, who knows?
A crime brutal and cunning,
Placing the guilt on another,
An implication, readily acceptable
By authorities, who knows?

Who knows what caused her mind to snap,
To send a car plunging into the depths,
With two innocent children trapped inside,
Followed by nine days of pretense and lies,
Who knows the pain, the grief of emotional
Helplessness, the misguided motivation of
Hopelessness that must have consumed her.
The children are safe in the arms of God.
Family friends, indeed the world is left stunned
With broken hearts, that questions, "why?"
And yes forgive, accept God.

CLASS POEM
1970

We have traveled this far, the road of knowledge,
Each carrying a special load.
Hoping by persistence and effort,
We could our characters mold.
For learning without character is useless,
So often we have been told.

We met "Carelessness" along the way,
Who attempted to turn us around.
We battled "Carelessness" day after day,
Finally we had him down.
For learning without character is useless,
With this motto we kept him bound.

On Latin Highway, "Helplessness" waited,
To ensnare us was his plan,
But with willing hands to aid us,
We soon this highway could scan.
For learning without character is useless
With this motto we can safely land.

We were warned to beware of "Aimlessness",
For he would creep up unaware,
As we traveled the "Road of Knowledge,"
We challenged him with a dare,
For learning without character is useless,
And ignorance with character is rare.

Don't think the journey was easy,
For we met others along the road,
"Temptation, Resistance, Procrastination, and Error,"
They all had a lure to unfold.

But learning without character is useless
And our characters we would mold.

We fear not the rest of our journey,
Nor what the future may hold,
To reach success there must be struggles,
And our characters we must mold,
This motto has made us bold.

Now that the time has drawn so near,
When we must part from you,
Principal, teachers and school mates dear,
We feel sadness too,
Dimming our joy, increasing our sorrow,
At thoughts of leaving you.

FIRST LOVE

Will I always of you think
As the years go by?
Will I the tears from my eyes blink,
When at night the stars will wink
As the years go by?

Will I find another love,
As the years go by?
When youth has died and old age is born,
Will I always for you yearn,
As the years go by?

Will you always remain the same
As the years go by?
In my heart the old refrain,
For me the one and only man,
As the years go by?

****

We weave our lives from day to day,
Entangling others in our thread,

We think life should go our way
With every thing fine with nothing to dread.

But life is a place of give and take,
Each of us must learn this lesson,
If we are true to the friends we make,
We gain life's fullest blessing.

A BIRTHDAY GREETING

It is your birthday, darling
May it be gay
Cheerful as birds
As they sing in May,
Long as God's arm stretched around the earth
May you enjoy many more
Such days of your birth

I THINK OF YOU

When the shades of night appear
I think of you,
In every song I hear your voice,
You are my one and only choice.
The gentle breeze seem to whisper your name,
The gay little birds are chirping the same.
Dear heart of mine believe me true,
I think of you.

In all my dreams, I see you still,
In your arms that held a thrill,
When dawn awakes, I shed a tear
In my dreams, you seemed so near
The tick of the clock as the minutes passes by
Keeps saying, "I love you,"
Believe me dear, the whole night through
I dream of you!

WELCOME

W   for words we learn to speak
E   for education which we seek
L   for loyalty, to Lafayette School
C   for courtesy, a very strict rule
O   for being orderly in all we do
M   for the meaniful things that we do
E   for efforts of everyone.

CHRISTMAS
1974

I looked at cards
That said too little
And some that said too much

This one is just about right
Have a Merry Christmas, that is "OUTASIGHT!"

I will always remember this Christmas,
The first we shared together,
Wasn't it fun?
The shopping and bustle,
The crowded stores,
Wrapping gifts,
Christmas Eve!
Going to church,
Meeting friends,
Singing carols,
And after midnight, saying "Merry Christmas."

SUNNING
1975

Up on the roof top,
Far from the crowd,
I seem to be floating,
Away on a cloud,

The sun rays,
Like a warm caress,
Eases and lulls me to sleep,
Smoothes and soothes my distress.

SARAH AND GEORGE LIVINGSTON
May 24, 1995

Dear Sarah and George,
Of your work I'm very proud,
I proclaim your fame,
Long and loud.

Continue to live
In love and peace
The good you have done
Will never cease.

WHEN IT IS OVER

Let me remember you not as you are,
But as you were in my dreams,
This elusion, I would not mar,
Though love has been crushed by faith it seems,
It is our destiny to depart.
How I failed you I wish I knew,
Was not my heart yours to own?

The tears I shed by your side,
When we talked night after night,
You saw, but ignored in your pride.
So long I struggled, so long I hungered,
The soul o f me, so misunderstood,
Filled with a nameless longing,
An endless yearning for love to
Transcend the flesh in utter completeness.
Thus to end so, this love,
We thought would last forever,
My eyes are dry; I can weep no more,
What we once shared,
Found its perfection only in me.

LOOKING BACK
JULY 1969

Life is a path,
We travel but once,
Yesterday has gone,
Tomorrow must come.

Look back if you will,
For the good it will do,
You cannot relive yesterday,
This rule is true.

Look back if you must,
For the good it will do,
Today is here,
To live, to do, to trust.

Look back if you are daring,
For the good it will do,
Were you generous and sharing?
Were you honest and caring?

Look back if you are wise,
For the good it will do,
Lessons from the past,
Should be your future guide.

A CHRISTMAS STORY
1976

A small boy gazed through the window pane,
He wanted the bright red candy cane.

His coat was thin and his shoes were worn,
He expected no toys on Christmas morn.

A few pennies, he had saved by doing chores,
And running errands for the stores.

He needed more money, where to start?
As he walked along, he was thinking hard.

"It is Christmas Eve," went through his mind,
I must think of something, there is not much time.

Suddenly, he saw among the throng,
A little old lady who didn't look strong.

Who was loaded so with parcels and bags,
Her shoulders were bent and her feet began to drag.

Forgetting his troubles, he ran to her side,
"I'll help you lady," he said with pride.

"Thank you," she said, "let's go to my car,
Just around the corner, not very far."

The car was there, warm and snug,
The lady was soon settled as cozy as a bug.

"May I," she said, "Give you a lift?"
And take this money as a gift.

His eyes were bright with unshed tears,
As he thanked the lady, He lost all his fears.

FRUSTRATION

Don't think about what cannot be,
A broken dream, shattered, can't you see?

Don't dream about what cannot be,
It is lost; it is gone, obliterated.

Overcome the sharp sting of tears, somehow,
Smile through the dull ache in you heart and vow,

To remember and remind you what is, must be,
Who you are, unique, different, set apart and set free.

With faith in God strive to mend your broken dreams,
Leave the vast ocean to seek your flowing streams.

Break clear, become oblivious to your troubled past,
Thank the Lord, you have found acceptance at last.

AN EPITAPH

Two little boys one sunny day,
Started to school and stopped to play.
Who can say what made them run,
It might have been fear but it might have been fun.

Two little boys with crushed bodies lay,
Still and silent on this day in May,
Two little boys this day departed,
From a life barely started.

Their parents and friends filled with grief,
What can we do to give relief?
Prayer is one answer and we plead,
For God's love and comfort to fill their need.

The faculty and staff feel your sorrow,
For two little boys who were borrowed,
From the Master's breast.
For a brief span before returning to rest.

AUTUMN LEAVES

Falling leaves that flutter
To the earth in coats of brown,
Do you regret having traveled from
Tree top to the lowly ground?

Falling leaves that rustle
To the ground as you descend,
Is the sound I hear a sigh you make
Or is it the cry of the wind?

Your life has been useful in its brevity,
After spring came the fall,
Don't you think, little leaf
Your life has helped us all?

When my season is over,
May I like the little leaf
Be able to say, I've lived my life,
And to some have given relief.

When my body shall lay
Once more in the clay,
Spirit of mine ascend
Know again, another spring.

MOTHER'S DAY

Mother's Day is the second Sunday of May, celebrated in the United States by honoring motherhood and giving presents to mothers. It was first observed in 1907 in Philadelphia and was established nationally in 1914 by an act of Congress.

SHE IS A MOTHER

In her arms they placed her child,
She welcomed the babe with an incredulous smile.
She is a mother.

From that moment, she had a vision,
The future depended on her decision,
She is a mother.

From kindergarten to a college degree,
She planned all a child could hope to be.
She is a mother.

She nurtured the child through tender years,
To love God, be honest, loyal and how to conquer fears.
She is a mother.

Coping with problems adolescence brings,
With God's help, overcoming all negative things.
She is a mother.

With adulthood, comes an empty nest,
An independent adult, proof she passed the test,
She is a mother.

Thank you Lord for all mothers,
She is different from all others.
You created mothers.

MARCH 21st

On the first day of Spring
Our hearts begin to sing,
In happy anticipation
Of the delights Spring will bring.

The bloom of the first flower,
The fresh smell from a soft shower,
The lush beauty of bright green leaves,
The soft touch of a gentle breeze.

Spring comes after the cold and snow,
Making all nature sprout and grow,
Children play and run and look,
Their world is like a picture book.

Spring comes after the glistening snow,
Our heavenly Father designed it so
All nature would awaken,
Winter cares would be forsaken.

Thoughts of Spring arouses us,
To new heights of faith and trust,
The beauty of all nature,
Is in the hands of our Creator.

SERVE OUR NEIGHBOR

S   Seek to do good for
E   Everyone everywhere, there is a
R   Real need to assist the
V   Victims of hunger, poverty, sickness.
E   Every place you go.

O   Opportunities are available to serve the
U   Under privileged, the unprepared to
R   Revive their lives and restore their faith.

N   Neighbors! Neighbors! Neighbors!
E   Every country. state, city and community
I   Invites us to be imitators of Jesus, to
G   Give generously of time talent and treasure.
H   Humbly and happily we can
B   Benevolence bestow on the broken lives of
O   Our neighbors near and far.
R   Religious faith is where we begin to
S   Serve! Serve! Serve!

A THANKSGIVING PRAYER

Lord of Goodness and Grace,
God of Mercy and Love,
Lord hear us when we pray,
You are always with us to point the way.

We give you thanks and praise your name,
Your Goodness is everlasting
From generation to generation,
Your truth through every age the same.

Approaching Thanksgiving and the
End of this millennium, we praise
In wonder, how timeless and mighty'
Is your greatness in the whole world!

How awesome and magnificent is your creation!
How miraculous are the laws of your universe!
How powerful is your name.
How abundant is your bounty!

Thank you, Lord for all the blessings
Bestowed upon us; forgive us our sins.
We beseech your compassion and guidance
As we enter the new millennium.
We rejoice and give honor to you, your son
And our Lord and Savior Jesus Christ.

Amen

RESPECT

Lyrical poems are not profound,
They might even be trite, you could say,
But the truths and values of which they speak,
Seem to be lost in the world today.

The strength of a poem is not its length,
Or the sweep of its content,
Its strength is revealed in the moment,
Heart or mind accepts its intent.

I think in rhyme,
I write because of pressures,
Pressures, insistent and persistent,
Whatever is its measure, pleasure or treasure.

I write of long lost morals
Flowing through my mind,
If any truth be there
The one who reads will find.

One moral value that is lacking
Is one of true respect,
A respect that begins with self;
Ends with what others can expect.

Mothers, fathers, sisters, strangers,
Neighbors, brothers, friends, teachers,
Babies, teenagers, seniors, cousins,
Aunts, uncles, grandparents, preachers.

Respect for authority,
Respect for the laws,
Respect for differences,
Even a government with flaws.

The more you show respect,
The stronger you grow.
When you respect yourself
Everyone you meet will know.

ONE DAY AT A TIME

The sparkle of dew on the grass,
The sight of a house wife polishing brass,
The warm breeze a bright cheerful sun,
The sound of children having fun.

So much to do on a summer day,
There is work to do yet time to play,
I made the beds and swept the floor,
Peeled potatoes while I watched a show.

Yes, I dusted furniture and did my work,
The most menial tasks, I did not shirk,
The sun was high in the sky by now,
The morning I dreaded had gone by some how.

Keep busy; take one day at a time,
Physical activity can help clear your mind,
However long it takes for the hurt to heal,
Live one day at a time, that's the deal.

ODE TO A BOTANIST

Proud peacocks strutted
In their private park,
The return of the wanderer home,
The sweet song of a meadow lark,
Stilled the urge to roam.
Thick ivy climbed on stately trees,
Peonies burst into bloom,
The buzz of busy bees,
Created beautiful music as I listened and walked.
That bright April afternoon.
Apple trees made a fashion show,
Dressed in white flowers,
Budding azaleas by the door,
Formed a fragile fragrant bower,
Sparkled from a recent shower.
The Judas Tree's heart shaped leaves,
Touched by wondering hands,
Fresh pine scented air this April day,
Created intoxicating perfume.
While peacocks strutted and waved their plumes
Sword shaped white Yuccas stood tall,
Surrounded by Rose petal Japanese Quince.
Poignant beauty everywhere.
A cushion of velvet soothed the feet'
The welcome sight of a quaint rustic seat
Purple wisteria growing in clusters,
At the peak of their luster,
Lithesome, long stemmed lilies,
Lifted their faces to the sun,
White and pure like a nun.
Breath taking loveliness everywhere.
A rare Botanist eager to share,
All the beauty that was there,

Proud peacocks in their private park,
Strutted and waved their plumes on an April afternoon.

OUR LOVE
February 9, 1996

A love so great, it fills my life,
Yet so gentle it keeps out strive.

A love that keeps my heart aglow,
But gives me space to think and grow.

A love that shares all my dreams,
Together we make a perfect team.

A love that always understands,
Always there, but never demands.

A love that watches over me,
And points out things I cannot see.

A love that's loyal and warm,
Quick to protect me from all harm.

A love that makes my days so bright,
Almost trouble free and burdens light.

A love that consoles me when I weep,
And prays with me until I fall asleep.

A love so quick to forgive, yet so generous in giving,
A love that makes our lives worth living!

I love you and wish you a happy valentine day.

LASTING LOVE
February 12, 1998

I loved you then,
I love you now,
I will love you
Throughout this life
And beyond.
I love you when we are happy,
When we are sad, I love you,
I love you when things go wrong,
My love will survive, because it is strong.
I will love you as we grow old and grey,
Just as I loved you yesterday.
My love for you
Will live on and on,
As long as there is life,
Memories and a life beyond.

RHYMING COUPLETS FOR COUPLES
February 14, 1998

You have been so silent here of late,
Please let me in, bring me up to date.

You haven't been out to dinner in quite a while,
Make a date, reserve a table, go dining in style.

He wants a vacation, you want to rest,
Talk it over and decide what is best.

You are busy, he wants to dance,
Forget the task and begin to prance.

He is sleepy, you are wide awake,
Let him sleep, go bake a cake.

Shopping with a friend, everything on sale,
Explaining a $150.00 bargain makes an amusing tale.

Whose turn to wash, whose turn to clean?
Working together, you make a perfect team.

You take turns reading, "The Upper Room,
You also take turns using the kitchen broom.

You both like doing and sharing all things together,
Going to church, reading, listening to music whatever!

Such incidents could go on and on!
But I'll take my seat and watch others perform.

A WINNER

Jesse Jackson, Presidential Candidate,
A Man of whom we are proud,
His face has been on T.V. screens,
As he articulates issues and dreams.

Dreams that involve not only blacks,
But the whole human race.
A man who stands strong and tall,
Whose ideals have a sound base.

By popular vote he is doing well,
As he speaks in every state,
The true percentage of electoral votes,
Is lost through the Democrate's mandate.

As he campaigns, we are with him,
Working right up to the "convention date,"
There, he will bargain for the best,
His decision will be the test.

He has made history in '84,
Our pride in him is great,
A brave pioneer, he has blazed a trail,
Where others who follow, will not fail.

MAKING UP
February 10, 1999

My love, I'm sorry
I was angry last night
How can you "put up"
With my changing moods?
My love, no one but you
Could forgive my stony silence
When you ask, "what is wrong?"
And receive no reply!
Only you can look into my eyes,
Make my heart glow,
Anger disappears,
Letting love show.

A WALL OF LOVE

My love is lasting
Like the lilting breeze
Which blows,
My love is loyal
It never loses
Love is life.

My love is over powering
It over whelms me
With its on going fervor
And out burst of passion.

My love has vitality,
Vigor and virtue
Which makes us victorious
Over any threat
To our happiness.

My love has eternal essence
Like faith in God
Shining stars in the sky
Rain drops that fall
A new born baby's cry
Or the sun in the sky,
My love is everlasting
In this life, in death and beyond

THE ABC'S OF LOVE
January 29, 1997

Love brings various things to different people. For some it's a life of happiness for others it's a major disappointment. Yet, Love is something we all long for- the perfect romantic, ne in a life time love. Why do some people find it the first time while others try but are never successful? Let's examine the ABC's of Love.

A   Do you show that special one admiration? Are you attentive and ardent?

B   Being there, being true, bold and brave through bad times as well as good times.

C   Children and church keep couples together. Either or both are strong common bonds.

D   Sharing duties and doing unexpected things for each other.

E   Use endearing terms- darling, sweetheart, etc.

F   Do you keep love fresh and renewed, by saying, "I love you," at least once a day?

G   Do you show gratitude for gifts? Are you generous with praise?

H   How about having prayer and meditation at meals.

I   What about interests, the shared ones and the individual ones? A couple needs both to make life exciting.

J   Do you jump to conclusions? Are you judgmental? Do you attempt to justify your mistakes or do you apologize quickly and willingly.

K   Have you kept your dreams, kicked up your heels once in a while? Do you kiss each other for no reason?

L   Do you like as well as love each other?

M   Do you have mutual friends? Do you motivate each

	other?
N	What about a pet name for that special someone? Do you discuss the news? Do you notice new clothing and make pleasing comments?
O	Are you on time for engagements? Are you organized and orderly in your habits?
P	Do you have patience when you become lost while traveling? Would you say, you are equal partners?
Q	Are you quick to forgive? Do you answer questions pleasantly?
R	Do you respect each other's privacy?
S	Are you able to separate and solve serious issues that affect both of you?
T	Is this the person you trust more than any other?
U	Do you really understand what is important to the other person? Are you unselfish?
V	What about vacations, do you plan and take them together?
W	Do you worship together? Share wonderful walks? Do you whisper whimsical words to each other?
X	Are you willing to go the extra mile?
Y	Do you keep your love young and yearning?
Z	On a scale from zero to ten how would you rate your love 0 – 10?

If you answered "Yes" to 20 or more questions your love is strong.

MARTIN LUTHER KING JR.
HE HAD A DREAM

He had a dream and saw
A future bright and clear,
His dream became a struggle for peace,
So his people could live without fear.
He had a dream of God's love,
Touching the hearts of all,
Working together for justice,
Removing the racial wall.
He had a dream of faith and hope.
A vision of a fairer land,
Where people stood united,
And prayed hand in hand.
He had a dream, the time is right
To march for freedom's light,
Peaceful protest is no crime,
But, segregation is a national blight!
He carried his dream to the mountain top,
He had a talk with God,
His dream, he knew could be his doom,
He had a dream that would not stop.
We have a dream now his voice is stilled,
To march on until his dream is fuffilled, this is God's will. To walk in dignity as he would, this is God's grace, To work on in peace as he did, this is God's love.

A BLACK CREED

THIS WE KNOW

About Black Pride, we hear so much,
Black Power, Black Awareness and such.
There are many ideas about Black Pride,
Helpful to stem the hate filled tide.
This will not take money or change in laws,
To eliminate certain racial flaws.
This will only require a little of your time.
To accomplish much and reduce crime.
Since Pride is free from outside help,
It is something each can develop himself.

THIS WE MUST CHANGE

Our black image is often spoiled,
By clothes not worn but only soiled.
Using language considered obscene,
Destroys pride and our race demean.
Senseless arguing and needless fighting,
Is also unseemly and personally blighting.
Where we live might be humble and old,
There is work to do on every threshold.

THIS WE CAN DO

Pick up the litter on the walk and in the yard,
There is nothing like neatness to win regard.
Wash the windows, mop the floors,
Solve domestic problems behind closed doors.
Let the grass grow under your feet,
Plant flowers on your street.
Show the children where and how to play,
Give them love and a bath every day.

We would flaunt this kind of pride,
As poverty becomes dignified.
Do not break windows, do not set fires,
This way we make the white men liars.
Budget money to the very last cent,
Use the rest wisely after paying the rent.
"How do we start and when?" you ask,
Now is the time to begin this task.

Not a penny more than we have will we need,
If each decides this advice to heed.
From the cradle on, instill a yearning,
To live with true dignity and learning.
Let us make a change before it is too late,
And the nation is destroyed by racial hate.
Most Black people will agree I know,
Wherever you are, let Black Pride show.

AWAKENING

We rode for miles
One winter night,
Just you and I
And around us lay
The virgin snow.

The night clear and cold
As we sped along,
The hum of the motor
The silent stars
And time stood still.

The houses we passed
Brilliant and gay with lights,
For it was Christmas,
This and your voice
Filled me with sweetness.

A sweetness I wanted
To share with you,
But I was strangely shy
And filled with awe
Of you and the silent night.

I was strangely shy
And could not break the spell
That held me to you
The hushed night
And the virgin snow.

Published in "Voices of Cleveland," Bicentennial Anthology of Poems by Contemporary Cleveland Poets 1996

EMPOWERING OUR NEIGHBORS

Our neighbors are empowered through missions,
To promote safe communities and schools,
Where people help each other,
Protecting, loving, understanding,
And respecting the rights of each citizen.

Our churches are enabled through mission money,
To deter crime, abolish drugs and alcohol, prevent violence,
Stop abuse and teach children peace and love.
Spread the good news of salvation, it is free,
Announce its power and win disciples for Christ.

Our schools are empowered to provide a safe place for learning.
Authorize our schools to become role models worthy of emulation,
Delegate neighborhoods to take charge of their environment,
Be responsive and responsible by helping eradicate the social ills
Threatening the moral fabric of God's people.

THE TOUCH OF MUSIC
May 2003

Music is a medium for universal communications.
It is like a smile easily understood.
Music evokes responses uplifting
The heart and soul of humanity.
Music stimulates the simplest or most complex mind.
To create and find from within
A blessing or an answer sought.

Music is therapeutic, calming and soothing the spirit.
If you are sad, it brings joy;
If you are ill, it gives comfort.
If you are angry, it brings peace.
If you are hurt and suffering it brings relief.
To the blind it gives sight.

Music is mission at work, on the heart and mind,
Proclaiming the Good News to all mankind.
Music has a lesson to those who listen.

SOUTH POINTE EMPLOYEE GIVES MORE THAN INFORMATION
September 30, 2002

Recently, I was at South Pointe where my husband was undergoing surgery. I had a long wait before I could see him. I spent this time in the lobby of the hospital. This is where I discovered Bernard a bundle of joyful energy. A slim African American male who is a ray of sunshine as he smiles and greets all those who are coming or going at the Information desk. He welcomes employees and doctors, nurses and staff by name. He has an encouraging word for patients as he directs them to the correct department. When they leave he has comforting cheerful words for he seems to remember them.

Although hundreds passed through during the long wait. He never stopped smiling. During a lull, he would come over and speak to those waiting for loved ones. Other times he would tidy the magazines and change the channel. He wanted everyone waiting to hear about their loved ones to be as comfortable as he could make them.

What amazed me also was how quickly he remembered my name and how to pronounce it when people I have known for years still have trouble saying it.

Bernard took one brief break at 11:15 A.M. and works from 6:45 A.M to 3:15 P.M. He has worked here only eighteen months but seems to know all the departments and how to guide people through the maze of construction work that is going on. Bernard formerly worked as an investigator for a law firm. He said, I have found my niche. I think God sent me here. At the end of the day, I feel wonderful because I have helped someone. Bernard is a native of Cleveland. In his spare time he is a vocalist spreading the message of God through song. Bernard is a jewel!

REFLECTIONS ON TIME

The approach of the millennium
Has me thinking about time
From many different aspects.
The time each of us lives on earth
Is melded in the flow that never ceases.
The minutes, the days the years pass swiftly.
Time waits for no one.
We all have equal time,
Equal time in a day,
To accomplish our goals,
By the skills we display.
There is a time to rejoice,
A time to be sad.
A time to speak,
A time to listen.
A time to celebrate,
A time to contemplate.
A time for action,
A time to be still.
A time to dream,
A time to make decisions.
A time to work,
A time to play.
Pray all the time,
God is sublime.

Now it's time for Cleveland Together to wish every one:
A glorious Christmas as you celebrate our Savior's birth.

A SUICIDE

She walked down a dimly lighted street,
There were no sounds of other feet.
The hour was late; the wind blew cold,
She had no job for she was old.
Old in an age old profession,
No one to turn to or hear her confession.
She opened her bag, one thin dime,
If on! she could turn back the pages of time.
Pulling her shabby coat tighter, she made her way,
Down the deserted street and who can say,
What must have been her thoughts?
What regret, what anguish, her memories brought'
Slowly, she approached the waterfront.
Deserted no longer, here and there, a drunk
Loitered or sprawled near one of the dives,
A place where she once worked to survive.
Music came through the open door,
A girl in a red dress danced on the floor.
She paused and peered into the smoky din,
A blatant reminder as a place of sin.
She looked into the faces of the motley crew,
The swiftly turned heads of the one she knew.
Spoke clearer than words can tell,
Her life had become a living hell.
She turned away from the faces of scorn,
Shabby and broke and her heart was torn.
With a mad despair, she heeded the call.
Of the deep, dark waters beyond the wall.

THANKSGIVING

Celebrate the Holiday,
Giving thanks and praise to God
For all his goodness and bounty.
While sharing delicious food with family and friends,
Remember the hungry and the homeless.

We enjoy the timeless traditions.
When at night, we kneel to pray,
We know God watches over us as we sleep,
Each morning he wakes us with a beep.
In our hearts we know every day is Thanksgiving.

HELPING NEIGHBORS HELP THEMSELVES

When words of love
Enter the heart; they
Bring joy and inspiration.
Kind words of hope,
Open the mind to explore all
Possibilities and solutions.
Extend a helping hand
For a short while.
Just as you would
Help a little child.
A child is nurtured
By love, teaching and hope.
Becomes strong and independent.
So might those who need
A helping hand, grow?
We extend a hand
To decrease strife.
And better a life!

MY PHILOSPHY OF EDUCATION

Education should prepare a person to live in a complex society such as ours. Education should enable one to live a well adjusted life, to decide on a vocation and to become a well adjusted member of society. To fulfill such an aim is very difficult to say the least because for one thing all people are not equally with learning abilities. Again, the readiness to learn even among children of the same age varies widely. Therefore, educators must be aware of these differences and the curriculum should be flexible and broad enough to reach the slow learner as well as the average, and the above average individual. All children should have the opportunity and training to develop to their fullest potential.

Education should give one the ability to cope with problems intelligently and constructively.

The aim of education should be to develop thinkers, nor mere rote learning of facts.

The processes and techniques of teaching should make the past understandable, the present livable and the future a successful possibility.

The field of education offers a continuous challenge from the administrative level down to the teacher in the class room. This is especially true in large urban areas with crowded class rooms and where the teacher must motive the culturally deprived.

I believe that a teacher must have in addition to techniques of pedagogy and knowledge, patience, kindness, and the understanding to secure the necessary rapport for successful teaching.

Each child is a unique individual and must be treated as such. Yet a teacher must instill the need for conformity to the rules of society to perpetuate desirable attitudes in each child.

BARACK OBAMA, ELECTED PRESIDENT OF THE UNITED STATES OF AMERICA

I never thought that I would live to see this day when American would whole heartedly elect a person of black heritage as President of USA!

I am so proud that as Americans, we have looked beyond color and recognize "the man", one who is capable, respected and who has won the trust, respect an love of not only America but people from around the world. America has come a long way when it recognizes that race and color made no difference in this election. The young, the mature and the oldest of citizens can be proud of themselves. This achievement the election of Barack Obama as President is a first. Although he has as much white blood as black, his color defines him.

This is a first and let us put our faith and courage and our hearts in building a country we can all be proud of. We can rejoice in being able to recognize ability and greatness and respond in a positive way.

President elect Barack Obama we are so proud of you. We can rejoice in people being able to recognize ability and greatness and respond in a positive way. We are proud so proud of this moment in history where America can stand tall and be proud of what America stands for. You are the President of all Americans, A staunch supporter of black and white, a president of all the, peoples of this great country.

America is behind you, beside you! You are in the front to lead the way!

NOTES

**OTHER BOOKS BY
SMALL FISH BIG SEA PUBLICATIONS**

The Bachelor's Fool & Life, Nothing but Drama
By Kimberly McKenzie
ISBN# 978-0-9801470-1-8
August 2009

The Black Mask
By Kimberly McKenzie
ISBN# 978-0-9801470-0-1
January 2008

www.ingramcontent.com/pod-product-compliance
Lightning Source LLC
LaVergne TN
LVHW091535060526
838200LV00036B/619